DATE DUE			

The Social
and
Psychological
Distortion
of Information

The Social and Psychological Distortion of Information

Charles K. West

Nelson-Hall [nh] Chicago

Library of Congress Cataloging in Publication Data

West, Charles K.
  The social and psychological distortion of information.

  Bibliography: p.
  Includes index.
    1. Communication—Social aspects.   2. Social
perception.   3. Senses and sensation.   4. Information theory.   I. Title.
HM258.W43   302.2   81–3941

ISBN 0–88229–616–7 (cloth)   AACR2
ISBN 0–88229–784–8 (paper)

Manufactured in the United States of America

10   9   8   7   6   5   4   3   2   1

Contents

Preface

In the past few decades, three revolutions have occurred which make this a new world. First of all, Western civilization has developed the wealth and other resources to employ unprecedented numbers of persons whose primary job is the production of information. As a result, massive amounts of information are being generated each day. Most of the world's information is less than fifteen years old. It has been estimated (Crane, 1972) that knowledge in physics, for example, doubles every eight years. There is little reason to expect that this is not the case for other areas. Second, electronic media have extended our ability to disseminate this information rapidly and totally. Third, computer technology has extended our abilities of analyzing this information. This growth is at times so rapid that we find it to be almost incredible. It was estimated, for example, that when the massive computer, ILIAC 4, was "plugged in" a few years ago it increased the world's computational capacity by 25 percent. Suddenly, we find that there is more information than we can effectively handle. Some of our basic institutions are asynchronic to these revolutions. Our governments were organized prior to these revolutions. The scientific establishments are designed to produce information, whereas the greater need now in most sciences is dissemination, sifting, and analysis.

The greatest problems, however, lie in the fact that people remain basically the same as information-treating mechanisms, intellectually and emotionally. More than ever before, we need to know about the informational interplay between human and human and between human and reality.

When information is so abundant and so easily and rapidly communicated, we should analyze its nature. How is it derived? How is it distorted? What role does human psychology play in its inception? What role does the human point of view play? What does human intention have to do with information? How do groups of persons influence information? We shall find that information may be distorted in many ways and that modern humankind needs a heightened sensitivity to self and to social groups before humankind can begin to handle rationally the modern information world.

The Organization of This Book

Chapter 1 is an overview of problems associated with large amounts of information and a discussion of some related philosophical issues. Chapter 2 is a very brief discussion of the psychology of human sensation and perception. In that chapter, I provide a general background on the research on human sensation. Chapter 3 is a discussion of how our knowledge influences information. The main idea is that we interpret events in terms of our previous learnings and how we have organized those learnings.

Chapter 4 is a discussion of the literature on how our values, attitudes, needs, and interests influence how we interpret events. In this chapter the reader will come to a greater understanding of the relationships between human intention and information construction, reception, and transmittal. Chapter 5 is a discussion of psychological research which has established the idea that social groupings can influence an individual's judgments and perceptions. Group conformity is very important in a study of information in that so much of our information is generated and communicated in group settings.

Students of language have long recognized that attributes of a given language may influence how persons conceptualize and represent reality. This will be discussed in chapter 6. In chapters 7 and 8, I discuss means of remediating information distortion. In chapter 9 distortion in science will be discussed, and in chapter 10, I attempt to analyze the implications of this monograph for institutions such as government.

Acknowledgments

Appreciation is expressed to these authors and publishers for granting permission to use the following published material.

Eliot, T. S. "The Rock," *Collected Poems 1909–1962*. London: Faber & Faber, 1934, and New York: Harcourt Brace Jovanovich, 1934. Harcourt Brace Jovanovich, Inc. for United States, its dependencies, and the Philippine Islands. Faber & Faber for other markets. Use of materials cited on p. 1.

Shaw, Bernard. "The Doctor's Dilemma" in Volume 1, *Bernard Shaw, Complete Plays with Prefaces*. New York: Dodd, Mead & Company, 1962. Permission granted by the Society of Authors, 84 Drayton Gardens, London, England on behalf of the Bernard Shaw Estate. Use of materials cited on p. 93.

West, C. K., and Foster, S. F. *The Psychology of Human Learning and Instruction in Education*. Belmont, CA: Wadsworth, 1976. Adaptation of Chapter 3 pp. 55–89 and use of table 5, p. 160. (See pp. 27–50 and p. 90).

CHAPTER 1

What Is Information?

Where is the wisdom we have
lost in knowledge?
Where is the knowledge we have
lost in information?
T. S. Eliot
from *The Rock*

The most pervasive characteristic of our world is that there is a massive amount of new and old information as well as instantaneous communication of that information. Today as never before we are bombarded with news and information from others while, at the same time, we have unprecedented abilities to create and transmit our own information to others.

The task of organizing information into what we consider to be knowledge—into what information means for us—is difficult enough when we have very little information. When we have massive amounts of information, some of that information is likely to be conflicting, and the task of formulating information into organized knowledge is greatly increased. Indeed, our structured knowledge can rapidly become obsolete with new information. This may be why McLuhan thinks that the person with a point of view is obsolete (McLuhan, 1965).

The extent to which information and its media have historically shaped our social institutions is not recognized.

Many of our major institutions—especially governmental—attained their present structures in times in which information was scarce and slowly communicated. Today the amount of information is massive and can be communicated practically instantaneously. It is a major technological-institutional asynchronism that the structure of our governmental institutions remains as though the amount of information and the rapidity of communication have not substantively changed for hundreds of years. Compare for a moment the information and communication technologies of 1776, when the American Revolution occurred, with the information and communication technologies of today. One of my hopes is that this short book will kindle an interest in research into how our institutions may be revised in terms of modern information and communication.

Information distortion is the very heart of propaganda. In our world of rapid communication, propaganda surrounds us like the air we breathe, and it may be the most vile form of pollution, for propaganda may inhibit our abilities and misdirect our actions in regard to all of our other problems. In understanding information distortion, we may be able to develop new ways of monitoring propaganda.

It is fortunate that instantaneous communication is a recent development. The despotic rulers we note in our history lacked the communicative devices of today. At least, total surveillance was not available to them. A citizen's every action was not knowable to the extent that is possible today, nor was it possible to bombard the citizen with constant propaganda. Many of the political leaders of today may lack absolute political power, but they do have available to them communicative technologies which are potentially just as powerful for control as is absolute political power.

In order to preclude this information control, we must

not only understand the propaganda which is transmitted to us, but we must also open our communicative technologies. By opening our communicative technologies I mean that traditional senders of information such as governmental and industrial institutions must be made more open to incoming information from citizens. We should not be satisfied, for example, until General Motors Corporation spends as much effort and money receiving information as sending information. Citizens must be viewed as sources of information as much as objects of information. For another example, our governmental agencies must be open to monitoring and surveillence for the protection of our rights. Citizens should have the same ability to obtain rapid and total information on governmental and industrial officials as these officials have for obtaining information about the citizens.

U.S. News & World Report (1978) estimates that 3.9 billion records on individuals now exist on computerized data systems in the federal government, and that most of them are available at the touch of a button. This does not include all the computerized records maintained by other governmental agencies, nor those which exist in industry and business. Bureaucrats or businessmen have immediate access to our records, our history, and our actions. Yet, obtaining knowledge on governmental and industrial personnel is a difficult and fragmentary process. Certainly, if we want information on a national legislator, for example, we must laboriously search many sources, and that information will be incomplete at best. Certainly, it will not be rapidly collected.

Problems of Large Amounts of Information

Increased information is generally considered advantageous. Rightly so. Because of this, it may seem puzzling that increasing the amount of information may increase the diffi-

culties of determining the implications of available information or of bringing information to bear on problem solving.
There are several considerations which make massive information problematic for us.

First of all, it may be inferred that most of us desire
certainty, exactness, precision, and a degree of absolute-
ness. We want fairly simple answers and answers which
have relative permanence. I believe there is an existential
yen for information which fits these specifications. Yet the
more we discover, the more we are faced with complexity
and conditionality. As Flavell (1977:1) states it,

> The really interesting concepts of this world have the
> nasty habit of avoiding our most determined attempts to
> pin them down, to make them say something definite and
> make them stick to it. Their meanings perversely remain
> multiple, ambiguous, imprecise, and above all unstable
> and open.

Certainly more information, information which increases
ambiguity and which reveals complexity, goes against this
human yen for simplicity, permanence, and exactness.
Propagandists and demagogues capitalize on this yen for
simplification. They offer people the simple, the panacea.
Those who try to reveal complexity are frequently ignored
in the process.

A second reason that a massive amount of information
may be problematic is that it increases the probability that
people will select from among the information and ignore
much of it as a result of the kinds of perceptual and
psychological selectivity which I discuss in chapters 2, 3,
and 4. Certainly, increased amounts of information increase
the possibility of our finding information which supports
our biases, attitudes, and pet theories.

A third problem is that of confidence in information.
Awareness that one may discover new information which

conflicts with present information may lead to increased uncertainty. The rapidity with which information is generated has to some extent influenced traditional relationships such as professor-student relationships in the university. Professors are aware that a student can go to the library after a lecture and locate information that was not covered in a lecture or even information which is in conflict with that presented. This may be one reason why professors are held less in awe—if they ever were—by students. The best expert may in fact be only the last person to go to the library.

Another problem with massive amounts of information is the recognized human limits in our ability to analyze the implications of information. Personal judgments are not likely to be accurate or complete when the items of information go beyond a certain number. Beyond that number most people cannot resolve conflicts and properly weigh implications (Meehl, 1954).

What Is Information?

What we know and sense about this sheet of paper—its whiteness, its size, its texture, and its other attributes—is information. One aspect of information is knowledge, but there are other aspects. Information is usually defined as knowledge communicated or received concerning some fact. The concept of information therefore includes the idea of communication—of some agent, usually a person, sending and some agent receiving. For the purpose of this book, sending and receiving always include human sensation and perception. Of course, we program computers to send and receive information, but the human element is involved in the original programming.

This definition of information includes the idea of knowledge which implies some form of human intellectual organizing and structuring as well as perception. It is this human organizing and structuring which gives rise to facts.

In other words, the facts about this page (which are communicated) arise not only out of the attributes of the paper
but out of my knowledge of paper in general, my intellectual organization and structuring, and my perception. It
may be said that before I can communicate the fact that
this paper is white, you and I would have to share some
knowledge about paper and about whiteness. Otherwise little
could be communicated. Otherwise the fact would be
unintelligible.

It could be said, then, that facts not only emerge from
some perceived object, but also that facts emerge from
knowledge and, further, from knowledge which is shared
by the sender and receiver. We must not only share this
knowledge, but we must also be able to sense and perceive
the attributes. What we sense not only emerges from the
attributes of the paper but also from characteristics of our
sensory and perceptual systems. That is to say, what we
know about whiteness depends as much on our visual
sensory system as on the attribute itself. Further, what we
sense about whiteness depends on our previous learnings
and knowledge. The sending and receiving of facts also
involve human sensation and perception. More will be said
about human sensation and perception in a later chapter.

The major point of this attempt at defining the concept
of information is that it is not a simple concept. Information is one of those concepts which in Flavell's (1977:1)
terms "perversely remains multiple, ambiguous, imprecise
and above all unstable and open." The idea of information
includes:

1. The existence of some object or event which has some
   attributes about which we communicate.
2. Some shared knowledge on the part of the sender and
   receiver—intellectual organization exists prior to communication.
3. Human sensation and perception.

4. Transmittal—sending and receiving—which also includes perception.

Information implies facts. But the term fact connotes truth and reality. In this monograph, information is data about the world which is a result of interactions between persons and persons and between persons and events. Information is the result of the interaction of the person (one's sensory perceptual systems and one's cognitive and affective schemas) with the culture, and with the events in the world.

It is important to emphasize that informational distortion and construction processes are interrelated. The processes involved in construction also induce distortion. Examining these processes is somewhat like looking at a coin: heads is construction, tails is distortion.

Information and Our World View

Embedded in communication about ideas, values, morals, and other objects and events is information. Information is news, the message. This book is about how information is developed and how it becomes confused and distorted. It is also necessarily about the concept of information and some related psychological and philosophical issues.

"Philosophy!" you say. "This book is supposed to be about the sociology and psychology of information, not philosophy!" You are right, but in the very beginning you may as well know that the questions about information distortion are also questions about the very nature of information, and that has everything to do with our philosophy— our world views, our statements about reality, knowledge, value, beauty, goodness, and morality. But most of all our models of reality and our ways of knowing are involved in questions about information.

If I believe that the world is an orderly place, I observe

sufficient instances of order to confirm my belief. If I believe that the world is basically irrational or disorderly, I see sufficient instances of this disorder to confirm this belief. If, to me, the world has a reality apart from me, then the information I have about the world has an order and a basic reality beyond me. If, on the other hand, I believe that the world is an illusion or construct of mine, then the information has different meanings, which are highly individual and private. If the world is disorderly or irrational, then information about such a world is irrational. Taking the irrational position to its logical conclusion, there is less reason to speak of the distortion of information, for then there is no invariant standard with which information may be compared. Perhaps there is no information in such a world, only noise.

In either of these cases the nature of information is at least as dependent on our knowledge about the world and the ways we have organized that knowledge as it is on the world itself. It is redundant but necessary to state that our information is about our knowledge of the world and not only about the world itself. Of course we always hope that there is some correspondence between social and personal knowledge and the nature of the world.

Subjectivism or Objectivism?

One of the most basic questions in the study of information and communication is whether we humans extract information, construct information, or both extract and construct information. The person with a subjectivisitic model of reality would argue that humans really construct information. Information in this view is not emergent from a real objective world and then extracted; it is constructed by the person. In this view the information is constructed by the subject (the person) and the word fact has little importance. Information is not always pure objective truth, consisting of the same facts for all persons for all times. In this view, any information is highly influenced by the person. In the strongest sense of subjectivism, all information is really distortion; all information is really disordered noise.

In contrast, the objectivistic view is quite different. In this point of view, information has at least the potential of being an accurate description of actual events in the real world. In this view, information has the status of undistorted truth, and there is a real world undistorted by human sensation and perception and undistorted by the subject, the person. Not only does this real world exist, but we have the skills to know it and to communicate it to others. In the objectivistic view, information is embedded in the world and extracted from that world. Knowledge is information, is fact.

Traditional Western philosophers have made a distinction which has helped us to understand subjectivism and objectivism. The distinction goes something like this. Human knowledge can be about two constructs: (1) events or objects themselves; and (2) the appearances of those events or objects. The question then arises as to which we can know about (or know the most about)—the events, or how those events *appear* to us. Western philosophy contains differences of opinion on this question. From a psychological point of view, it would seem that knowledge is largely restricted to what appears through human sensation and perception. If we return to the item of information "this paper is white," what we may really be saying is that this object appears to me as paper and, further, appears to me as white. A clearer example might be an item of information such as "the president of the United States is moral and ethical." All of my own subjective attitudes and perceptions then come into play about the nature of moral and ethical conduct in general and the extent to which the president acts in terms of my subjective attitudes. If the actions of the president are known to some extent by you, and I said to you that the president is moral and ethical, I would be revealing as much about me—my notions of the nature of moral and ethical behavior—as I would be revealing about the president. It is valid to contend that the attribute "white" (referring to paper) also communicates my knowledge and judgments about whiteness to the same extent as my contentions about morality. Both really refer to my statements about how things appear to me. Both may be taken as items of information, yet both are about the appearances of events or things.

Objectivism is the ordinary common sense view that what one senses is the absolute fact, the actual reality undistorted and true. This commonsense point of view often seems accurate, for it provides its own support in a circular way. That is, if I say that this paper is white and you ask for evidence the basic act of proof is to look again. That is, you observe and assume that observation provides evidence. However, once we examine that process of proof of the fact, we find that the proof is circular; it is simply a restatement and not really proof. That is, on the first occasion I say that the paper is white because it appears as white. For proof you or I look again, and once again it appears as white.

Once we examine the circularity of the commonsense view, we have at least two beginning points. We can question both the knowers (in philosophical terms, the subjects, or you and I) and the object (the event, or the paper). In philosophy, the examination of the nature of knowledge (or information) frequently begins with the study of subject-object relationships. Once we question the commonsense point of view, we raise questions about how the nature of the subject (the knower or person) may have influenced the information obtained; but we also raise questions as to aspects of the object other than its appearances. The great philosopher Alfred North Whitehead resolved subject-object relationships in a relativistic way (as I will in this book) by arguing that knowledge is the subjective interplay between subject and object (Whitehead, 1933:177). According to subjectivistic relativism, information is embedded in the relationship between the knower and that which is to be known. That is to say that information is a relative function of the person's interaction with some object. The nature of the person determines the nature of the information as much as does the nature of the object.

Thus, the relativistic view of knowledge, or information, recognizes that information is relative to human nature as well as relative to appearances of events. Variances of an informational nature are not solely a function of the lack of careful observation—as claimed by objectivists—but are a function of the nature of observation itself. In the relativistic view, an item of information derives its status and its existence from its relationship to the person and from its relationship to all other information. When we look at one event we find it connected to every other aspect of the universe. It is impossible to know an object in its own right. We know it in its interrelatedness to other objects and to us. Items of information exist in vast and apparently unlimited webs. Pull one piece of the webbed fabric, and other pieces are attached and thus influence information extraction and construction.

Problem Solving, Information Gathering, and the Psychological and Social Distortion of Information

Information extraction and construction is integral to problem solving. Dewey (1910) conceptualized problem solving as consisting of several stages. Basically these stages are (1) selection and statement of the problem, (2) gathering of information, (3) trying out solutions based on that information, and (4) selecting the best solution in terms of how the trials worked out.

Persons use some information at each of these stages. We become aware of a particular problem as a result of information (stage 1) and the three remaining stages involve information directly.

In Figure 1–1 I have outlined many of the sources of information distortion. I include a detailed discussion of each of these sources of distortion in later chapters of the book. I present the sources here in Figure 1–1 for an overview as well as to mention that many of these sources of information distortion influence each of the four problem-solving stages.

Information distortion may begin even at the point of selecting a problem. We may conceptualize that there is an apparently unlimited number of problems in the world. Psychological and social factors (see B, C, D_1, D_2, E, F in Figure 1–1) affect the selection of a problem from among all of the potential problems. As persons select and develop information pertinent to the selected problem, these same six factors continue to bias the information about the problem. For example, group norms or group ideology (D_2) may influence not only problem selection but also information selection about that problem. This pervasive interaction between problem solving and information distortion processes seems to me to apply to all of us to some degree. This is so even for scientists who we may think are free from information distortion.

Scientists also have their ideologies and are vulnerable to the same distortion phenomena. Kuhn (1970), for example, has shown how scientific revolutions can occur as the ideology (paradigm in Kuhn's terms) of science changes. It may take decades or even centuries for the paradigm or ideology to shift so that scientific change may take place. This issue and others are also raised about science, by

A	B	C	D₁	D₂	E	F
An apparently unlimited number of problems and events in reality.	Human sensation can sense only certain **types** of events in only limited ways.	A person can perceive only a limited number of events (B) at any moment in time.	A person's knowledge and emotions partially determine which of the events in C are noted. Interpretations of C are made in terms of knowledge and emotion.	A person's perceptions of C may also be influenced by group norms and social pressure.	Intentional bias as a person consciously selects from D_1 and D_2 that which will be communicated to others.	The receiver of information (provided by others) will return to step C and all other steps (C, D_1, D_2) may be repeated.

Figure 1–1.   **Steps in the psychological and social distortion of information.**

Remmling (1967). Distortion in science will be discussed in detail in Chapter 9.

A major thesis of this book is that there is an element of subjectivism in all information and that we must recognize this subjectivism as we consider information and the communication of that information. It is through the study of this subjectivism that we may modestly begin to answer T. S. Eliot's question—a most poignant one for modern man —"Where is the knowledge we have lost in information?"

CHAPTER 2

Human Sensation and Perception and the Frame of Reference

One of the primary considerations for understanding information is stimulation. A stimulus is any event which initiates activity in an organism. For a human there are two sources of stimuli, internal and external. External stimulation occurs when some event outside the person activates one of the five sensory perceptual systems as discussed by Gibson (1966): kinesthetic—balance, the sensing of movement and position; auditory; haptic, or touch; tasting or smelling; and visual.

In the most simple way of stating it, each of these senses transmits mechanical or electro-chemical impulses to the central nervous system as they are activated by energy variations in the environment and in the person. For example, in the case of seeing, light variations in the environment induce impulses in the eye. What the central nervous system receives is induced by the eye and its associated nerve cells. Roughly speaking, what the central nervous system receives by way of stimuli comes from the sensory organs and not directly from the environment. We can know only in a limited way how what the central nervous system receives corresponds with what is happening outside the organism. Does the environment appear to us as it really is? I doubt we can ever really answer this question. It is my position that it is horrendously naive to assume that what appears to us has a one-to-one correspondence with what is really "out there" in reality. Again the philosophical distinction between events themselves and the appearances of those events is both convenient and necessary.

We might ask how humans and other organisms survive as they interact with their environment if there is not a close correspondence between the actual nature of the events in the environment and what appears to the senses. Adaptation and evolution imply that the sensory perceptual systems must provide organisms with functionally accurate environmentally based messages. Perhaps the key is that the sensory perceptual adaptations are functional. They provide messages which enable the organism to use facets of the environment and to respond more or less effectively to it. It would appear that a species could not survive without this functional relationship. However, a functional relationship does not necessarily imply a one-to-one relationship. The visual pictures we get from the world may enable us to survive in the world without the picture being in a one-to-one relationship to it. A fox gets a view of its prey, and this view together with other skills of the fox enables it to capture its food. Thus, its vision is functionally adaptable, but the view may not be a complete and accurate view of the prey.

Selectivity of Stimuli

The basic characteristic of human sensation for the purposes of this book is selectivity. If all the potential stimuli in an environment actually initiated activity in the person, that person would be so overwhelmed with sensory perceptual input that rational action would not be possible. Consider my situation as I write this. I feel the pencil with my finger (I am forced to stop writing as I consider each in turn), the pad with the heel of my hand, the desk with my wrist, my chair arm with my elbow, the seat of my chair, and the floor with my foot. I see the words, the pad, the pencil, and part of my desk in its disarray. To my right through the window I see the white snow and dismal fog of an Illinois winter. I hear my metal mobile, and the soft roar of the heating fan, the buzz of my desk lamp, some students talking and others walking outside my door, not to mention the typewriter. These are only a small fraction of the potential external stumuli which can command my attention—and these of course did command my attention as I selected them. If I sensed all of these instantaneously the world would be total confusion and everything would become disordered noise. Worse than that, I would never finish this chapter.

Perhaps adaptive processes have forced certain species to be thoroughly selective. We must use partial stimuli in order to use any. The selectivity is functional. The first aspect of selectivity is the fact that of all those environmental events we can physiologically sense, we can attend to only a few of them at any given moment through sequential focusing.

Our sensory-perceptual physiology provides another kind of selectivity. We know that there is much going on in the world which we cannot physiologically sense or perceive. We can hear only a small range of sounds. In seeing, we respond to or use only a small portion of the electromagnetic energy spectrum. Visible light is part of a much larger continuum of energy including such longer-wave emanations as infrared, microwave, radio waves, and so on and such shorter-wave emanations as ultraviolet and cosmic rays. We can sense directly only a small portion of this spectrum. Of course, we can build tools which help us to conceptualize and understand these emissions, but the information from the tools has to be interpreted in other terms. We still cannot totally visualize or imagine how a world would appear through these energy emissions.

Up to this point I have discussed two kinds of selectivity.

First are the physiological limitations of our senses. Secondly we can only attend sequentially to portions of the potential stimuli surrounding us. We could graphically represent these kinds of selectivity in the following way (see Fig. 2–1). Let A represent the apparently infinite amount of events which seemingly exist in the universe; let B represent the portion of the universe which we can physiologically sense; C then pictorializes the limited number of potential stimuli to which we can attend at any given moment.

This selectivity counters the image of the person as a passive receptor of stimuli. A more accurate image of the sensory person is that the person is an active hunter of stimuli—the person selects, ignores, and focuses on an already limited portion of potential stimuli in the universe. The universe does not represent itself indiscriminately to the person as a passive receptor.

Habituation, Inhibition, and the Herenandez Peon Effect

There are three known ways in which selectivity is attained. The first is habituation. Habituation is a process of becoming so accustomed to a continuing stimulus that it apparently is not noticed. My neon desk lamp has a buzzing but I rarely notice it; one of my colleagues cannot tolerate it during our discussions. This is also true for many of the stimuli I mentioned earlier—the feel of the pencil, the chair as I sit on it, the feel of the floor on my feet, and so on. I have habituated, and these stimuli are not noticed. This enables me to attend to the stimuli I choose.

The second way selectivity is attained is through lateral inhibition. Nerve cells in many parts of the body exist in cables, many of them running laterally toward the central nervous system. Physiologists have found that if one of these elongated nerve cells is transmitting impulses,

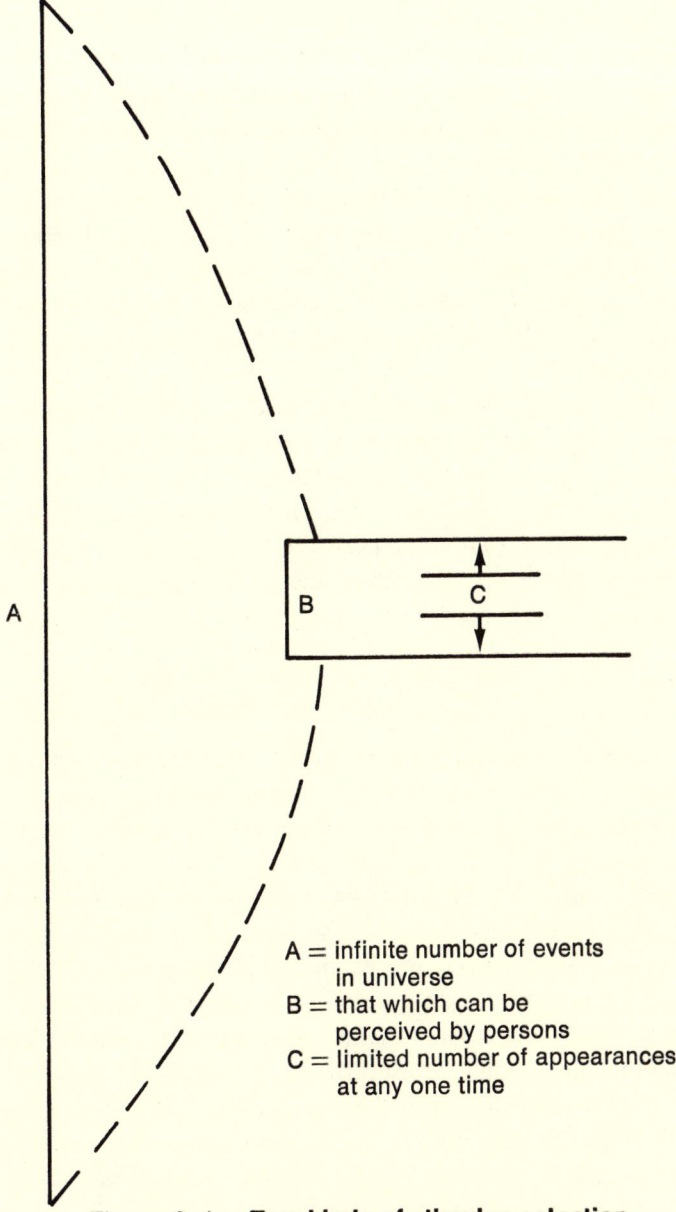

A = infinite number of events
in universe
B = that which can be
perceived by persons
C = limited number of appearances
at any one time

Figure 2–1. **Two kinds of stimulus selection.**

nearby cells in the cable are reduced in their capability to transmit other impulses. This has an overall effect of reducing the number of stimuli transmitted toward the central nervous system.

A third way selectivity is attained—and perhaps the most interesting from a psychological point of view—is the Hernandez-Peon effect. In Hernandez-Peon's (Hernandez-Peon et al., 1956) famous investigation, minute electrodes were surgically implanted in the central nervous system and in the auditory nerve cells of a cat. When a clicking sound was made, the neural record indicated that impulses traveled through the auditory nerve cells into the brain. A jar containing two mice was placed before the cat. When the clicking sound was made near the cat's ear, the impulse appeared in the auditory nerve cells, but not in the brain. Interpretations of this surprising finding are speculative, but it would appear that visual stimulation actually suppressed the auditory stimulation to such an extent that the auditory stimulus was not received in the brain. Incidentally, related effects have been found with chimpanzees.

As the stimuli impinge upon the person, they are also selected and rejected in terms of learning. That is to say, once we consider the stimulus impulse as having reached the person, learning is a possibility. The stimuli themselves should simply be viewed as energy exchanges. It is through learning and experience that they come to have any meaning. Consider vision, for example. It apparently requires much learning before the color, shape, and shade variations which are seen begin to make sense to a person. Adults who have been blind from birth and who suddenly, through surgical treatment, gain their sight report that their visual world is quite confusing and meaningless. It takes quite a bit of learning and experience before their visual stimuli begin to make sense. The necessity of learning is probably true for the other senses as well.

So far in this chapter, I have written about the selectivity of external stimuli. At the very beginning of this chapter I mentioned that there are two sources of stimuli—external and internal. A human has a very high capacity for internal stimulation. In the next section I will discuss the notion of the human frame of reference, the fact that it generates stimuli, and the fact that it also contributes to the selection of external stimuli. The frame of reference is a major factor in the study of information, since the frame of reference is a major factor in creating information from stimuli. Stimuli are only the raw products from which a person, through a frame of reference, creates information.

The Frame of Reference

The idea of the frame of reference is only a convenient way of attempting to represent a person's history, experiences, learnings, needs, and, in a sense, aspirations. If we wish to explain the behavior of most living organisms, we find that instinct plays an important and perhaps the major role. But, if we wish to explain human action, we seem to be primarily concerned with learning and not with instinct.

This is not to say that the frame of reference is limited to learning; the frame of reference also includes genetic factors. For example, many of our needs (a part of the frame of reference) are determined genetically. The frame of reference is nothing more than a convenient way of conceptualizing a person's past learning and part of his inherent nature. However, the theory is based on a great many empirical studies, as you will see later. A frame of reference has six components: concepts (fragmented, separate portions of knowledge); structures (organized bodies of knowledge); affects (mainly feelings, dispositions, and temperaments); needs (deficiencies); values (the person's ideas of worth); and interests. These interrelated components of the frame of reference will be discussed in greater detail in chapters 3 and 4. For the moment, we need only notice that frames of reference serve two functions insofar as information is concerned. First, they partially determine what the person senses and perceives of the external universe and create information from the sensations; second, they internally stimulate the person.

These two informational functions are presented in Figure 2–2. Line B represents that already limited and selected region of stimuli noted in Figure 2–1. These stimuli potentially impinge on the person. The frame of reference acts as a filter, and certain stimuli are selected. Interpretations are based on the frame of reference. The six components also generate information themselves. This general picture of the role of the frame of reference is discussed in detail in the next two chapters.

It may be helpful to discuss Figure 2–2 in some detail. The selectivity discussed in the first few pages of this chapter seem by and large to be based on physiological or neurophysiological processes. Selectivity and distortion emerging from the frame of reference seem to be primarily psychological, that is, based primarily on the previous learnings of the individual. As stated earlier, events which occur may become stimuli and may initiate some activity in the person. Whether or not the activation occurs may depend largely on the frame of reference. Each frame of reference component acts as a filter on the potential stimuli. Of course, this selective or filtering effect can be overcome by certain powerful stimuli. For example, if I am busily writing I may not hear a soft sound, but if someone screams in my ear, not much screening occurs.

Screening or filtering effects are represented by the symbol a. Information is not derived from an event unless the filter admits the associated stimulus. The frame of reference also generates impulses, or internal stimuli, which are represented by the symbol b. Our actual behavior will

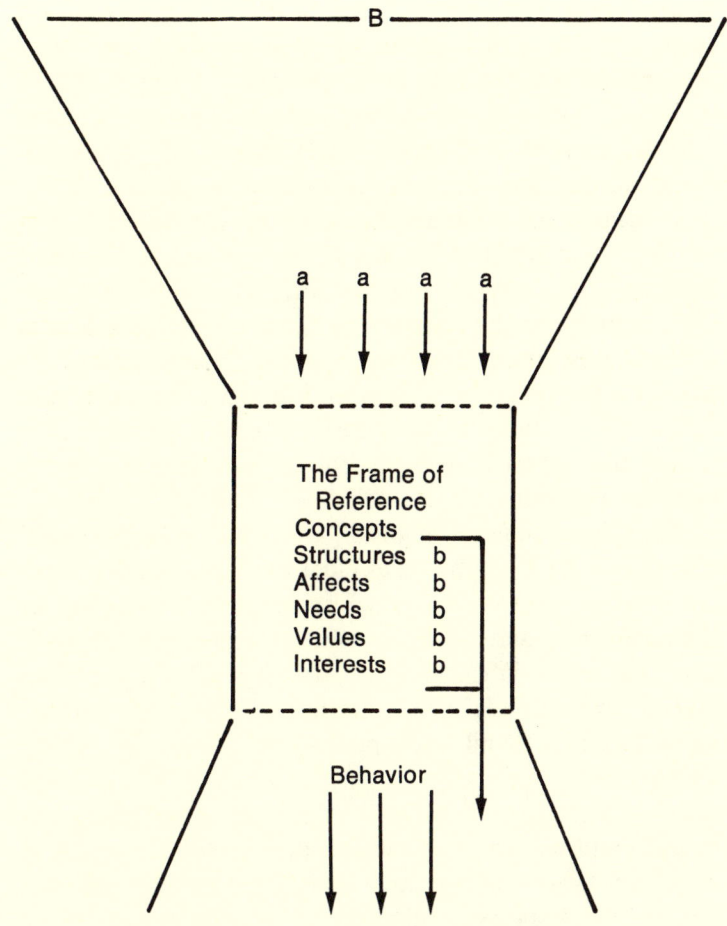

Figure 2–2. **The selective (a) and generative
(b) effects of the frame of reference.**

be a function of either the filtered stimuli (a) or the self-
generated internal stimuli (b). Behaviors which are informational in nature may be either filtered or self-generated

in origin. Yet, in most instances, both are strongly influenced by the frame of reference.

The frame of reference is not to be considered as static. It should be seen as constantly changing and evolving. New experiences can modify any of the components—for example, new information can modify conceptual and structural components (Anderson and Ortony, 1975). Nevertheless, a person's frame of reference is an important determinant of that person's behavior, and, as will be seen, it also exerts powerful influences on perception, learning, memory, and thinking.

This particular theory, the psychological paradigm of frame of reference, may suggest to the reader a general picture of stalwart individuals isolated from others and unaffected by other people. Such a picture is inaccurate for at least two reasons. First of all, we share a great many of our experiences (the building blocks of the frame of reference) with others—so in that respect we are all somewhat alike. Second, there is ample evidence that an individual's perceptions and judgements are strongly influenced by the perceptions and judgements of others. This latter point will be discussed in detail in chapter 5.

Conclusions and Summary

The emphasis on informational distortion and selectivity masks the positive generative and constructive aspects of perception. While perception is selective as a result of the neurophysiological and psychological dynamics discussed, perception is also generative and constructive. Decades of research from Bartlett (1932), Hebb (1949), Gibson (1966), Neisser (1967), and many others emphasize this. For example, Hebb (1949) coined an analogy which sums up the constructive dynamics of perception very well. He thought that the perceiver is like the paleontologist who locates a few bone fragments of a long extinct dinosaur and reconstructs the entire form. The perceiver uses the sensation by projecting learnings on it and derives its meaning just as the paleontologist projects his knowledge on the bone fragments. Whatever meanings are derived from a perceptual act are thus constructed through the interaction of the knowledge of the person as well as other attributes and the sensation. These meanings then become that which is learned. They become the information derived.

CHAPTER 3

How What We Know Distorts Information

The formulation of experience . . . is determined . . . by the basic concepts at people's disposal. . . .
Susanne K. Langer
Philosophy in a New Key

We have seen that a person's frame of reference consists of both cognitive (or knowledge) and emotional components. In this chapter, we will discuss how the knowledge components of the frame of reference influence how we perceive and think about reality. The knowledge components of our previous experiences may be seen as represented in the mind in terms of parts and wholes, or concepts and structures. These may also be seen as the information a person already has as the person attempts to gain new information. Both the concepts (parts) and structures (wholes) are important as a person attempts to extract new information. These parts and wholes are only relatively stable in the open-minded person —that is they may be changed and reordered in terms of new information (Anderson & Ortony, 1975). These two components are also closely related to each other.

Concepts

The term concept is usually defined as an object of awareness together with its meaning or significance. A concept implies a rule for categorizing objects according to similarity or commonness among them and is thus, to a degree, abstract and general. The term table is the name of a concept. Certain similar characteristics of objects such as tables are shared. Our common agreement about these shared characteristics enables us to recognize, characterize, and differentiate among individual objects and to communicate our awareness to one another.

Much of a person's knowledge is conceptual in nature. Concepts are abstract by their very nature and by the symbolic nature of knowledge and memory. Concepts can be said to represent degrees of abstractness; thus "cow" is less abstract (closer to an instance) than is "mammal." Concepts like "honesty" and "democracy" are, of course, more abstract than "hardness" or "tabular." Previously learned concepts influence the ways a person senses, perceives, and thinks about new phenomena. Psychological research from a variety of points of view support this contention. Judson, Cofer, and Gelfand (1956) had subjects learn lists of words in serial order prior to solving Maier's (1930) two-string problem. This problem involves bringing two strings together which are suspended from a ceiling so far apart that subjects could not grasp one string and then the other to bring them together. One solution consists of making a pendulum of one string by tying some object to the end and setting it in motion, then bringing the other as close as possible and grasping the pendulum as it swings near. Those subjects whose list of words included the words "rope, swing, pendulum" in that order were more efficient at solving the problem than the control group. Maier (1930) demonstrated the difficulty of this problem. Few of Maier's subjects solved the problem without some guidance. This study illustrates the impact of previous learnings in the form of concepts on problem solving.

Another related series of experiments have been conducted on the influence of labels on recognition. Several investigations support the idea that the provision or formation of a label prior to a recognition task helps recognition (Katz, 1963; Campbell and Freeman, 1955; Gaydos, 1956; and Kurtz and Kooland, 1953). Some labels may be considered to be names of concepts if they come to stand for a class of objects with some common characteristics.

Cantril (1950) and Ittelson and Cantril (1954) discuss the role of experience and knowledge (much of which is conceptual) in establishing expectations which are of primary importance in interpreting stimuli. A person's experience (including concepts) also has an impact on the recognition of stimuli (Bagby, 1957). Bagby used a stereoscope, in which one picture was presented to the left eye and another to the right eye. In one pair of slides a picture of a baseball player was presented with the picture of a bullfighter. Most North Americans tested recognized the baseball player whereas most Mexicans recognized the bullfighter. This study indicates that knowledge obtained over an extended period influences sensation and perception. A predisposition to perceive in one way over another is termed a perceptual set.

The study of Judson, Cofer, and Gelfand (1956) as well as other investigations—(Haselrud, 1959; Saugstad, 1955; Immergluck, 1952; Carmichael, Hogan, and Walter, 1932; Murray, 1933; Siipola, 1935)—indicate that such sets may be induced just prior to the experimental period and that these sets influence sensation, perception, and cognition. Bruner and Minturn (1955) induced expectations in subjects to see either numbers or letters. To subjects expecting letters of the alphabet "13" was seen as a "B," and to those expecting numbers "B" was seen as "13." Bugelski and Alampay (1961) presented two groups of drawn figures to subjects. One group consisted of drawings of animals, and the other group consisted of drawings of faces of people. One drawing was included in both groups. If the common drawing was presented with drawings of animals it was seen as a rat; if presented with drawings of human faces it was seen as a person's face.

Structures

The term structure is used here in two ways. First, the various sciences, arts, and disciplines each contain structures of which we may be aware. In this sense, a structure is a conventional and usually logical way of organizing and interrelating information or concepts included within that science, art, or discipline. These social conventions are shared by many persons within that field of knowledge. Structures of this type are learned along with other information and concepts. Rules of grammar are examples of this type of structure in a language. The taxonomic systems in biology and zoology are other examples. Structures of the second type are those personal, relatively individualized, ways of organizing and interrelating information, phenomena, and concepts which the person encounters in present experience or in memory. Each of these types of structures includes many concepts and is based on content.

It is widely accepted that one's knowledge of the structures within a subject matter field influences ability to learn new material in the field. Ausubel (1968) distinguished two kinds of meanings which correspond with two types of structures: logical meaning and psychological meaning. Logical meaning is symbolic in that it consists of nonarbitrary and substantive relationships within the material. Psychological meaning is the product of an individually meaningful learning experience. The person idiosyncratically develops psychological meaning by nonarbitrarily and substantively relating potentially logical and meaningful material to relevant ideas within the person's cognitive structure. Material can only be meaningfully learned when material is logical as well as relatable to the person's cognitive structure (Ausubel, 1968:37–45). Ausubel states that one of the crucial factors within the person which influences one's learning ability is the person's cognitive structures:

> Since subject-matter knowledge tends to be organized in sequential and hierarchical fashion, what one already knows in a given field, and how well one knows it, obviously influences one's readiness for related new learnings. (1968: 26)

Ausubel (1960) has demonstrated the usefulness of providing general structures (logically meaningful material) and advance organizers which mediate between what students already know and that which students are to learn.

Numerous studies illustrate the influence of structures on learning, retention, transfer, and problem solving. Reynolds (1966) concludes that organized perceptual structure may aid new learning. Other research (Postman, 1954) indicates that learning rules of organization facilitates rote learning. Other studies (Ausubel, 1960; Ausubel & Fitzgerald, 1961; 1962; Merrill & Stolurow, 1966) indicate that providing general organizers which correspond to ideas previously existing will facilitate both learning and retention of meaningful material. When the person has a structure to which the material can be anchored or subsumed, learning and retention is promoted (Ausubel, 1968). Studies by Judd (1902) and by Overing & Travers (1966) also indicate that making a general principle available will help transfer. Other studies (Katona, 1940; Hilgard *et al.*, 1953; Hilgard *et al.*, 1954) indicate that knowing a general principle will result in better problem-solving performance on a class of problems than will memorizing the solution.

During every waking moment, humans are exposed to numerous, somewhat unrelated bits of potential information or stimuli. The number of unrelated stimuli which can be retained is limited, and Miller (1956) suggests that 7 ± 2 is the limit. What happens when the number of stimuli to which one is exposed and is expected to remember exceeds the span of retention? Evidence is quite clear that humans can develop organizing schemes to aid memory. Bousfield (1953) reports "clustering"; Miller (1956) describes "chunking"; Jenkins and Russell (1952) talk about "structuring"; Mandler (1966) reports "organizing"; and Katona (1904) describes "grouping." The organizing scheme enables one to extend the number of stimuli remembered. Miller (1956) argues that the limitation holds with qualification for making judgments about or discriminating among the bits. He also speculates that this limit extends to perception of the bits. Should this be a valid speculation, the structures not only aid memory but also aid and extend the number of discriminations among the bits of potential information. Structures should also enable one to perceive and discriminate attributes of an object and to increase or limit the number and quality of attributes perceivable. A person encountering a large number of potential items of information is able to discriminate and remember from five to nine of the items (or whatever that individual's limit is for that task) within some organizational scheme. Each of the discriminations made within the original organizational scheme may become a basis for expanding the limits of the discrimination and for extending perception of the bits and for aiding both memory and recognition.

Generally speaking, the human ability to develop efficient structures for the organization of bits of information increases with age, up to maturity. The basis of the structures used generally become more seminal and symbolic during middle childhood. Olver and Hornsby (1966) and Bruner and Olver (1963) note that younger children group arrays through imagery, that is, they are dependent upon moment-to-moment perceptual vividness. After about age six, most children begin to relate items in the array symbolically or linguistically. A child under six tends to structure along the lines of perceptually obvious characteristics of color, shape, or size. An older child tends to structure according to function and symbolic commonness.

Investigations such as these lead one to surmise that a person's thinking and learning abilites depend primarily upon linguistic skills and ability to organize and structure, two highly related sets of skills. According to the eminent Swiss psychologist Jean Piaget (see Piaget and Inhelder, 1969), the person's repertoire of structures is of primary importance in cognition. Piaget identifies three classes of structures which he terms "schemata": groupings, lattices, and groups. Groupings are those systems of simple or multiple class inclusion typical of children at the stage of concrete operations (roughly between the ages of seven or eight to age eleven or twelve). The following description of one of Piaget's experiments should provide the reader with some grasp of a structure which an older but not a younger child will use to solve a problem. The subject is told that a substance G, when combined with liquid from two of four beakers of different liquids, will produce a yellow solution. A child younger than 11 or 12 will set out to discover in a random fashion which combination will produce the yellow solution. The child will attempt various combinations in an unsystematic manner—for example by adding G + 1 + 4, G + 3 + 4, G + 1 + 2. There is no order to the combinations, and the child may repeat combinations. The random approach takes longer. An older child may use a combining system which will result in systematically trying all possible combinations in an orderly fashion—by adding G + 1 + 2, G + 1 + 3, G + 1 + 4, G + 2 + 3, G + 2 + 4, G + 3 + 4, one of which will be the

correct combination (Inhelder and Piaget, 1958). Impos-
ing such structures on problems enables the person at the
stage of formal operations (roughly 11 or 12 or older) to
solve problems quickly and efficiently.

According to Piaget, the person's repertoire of structures
increases in developmental stages. At the stage of concrete
operations the structural repertoire is limited and these
structures enable the young person to deal primarily with
concrete instances rather than higher level abstractions.
The person can perceive and operate on the concrete, but
cannot operate on the potential—that which the here and
now might imply logically. Upon reaching the stage of
formal thought, operations and structures are more numerous and complete, and the person is able to visualize and
operate upon the possible or the potential. An older person
can escape the perceptually concrete, is not bound up in the
limits of the concrete, and can fit the more symbolic dimen-
sions of problems and problem arrays into even more
sophisticated structures.

Anderson, et al. (1977) had persons who had different
backgrounds (physical education vs. music) read the same
passages and take multiple choice tests on the passage
material. Subjects' backgrounds strongly influenced their
interpretations of the prose passage. These investigators
suggest that the schemata are imposed on messages or in-
trude on the message without any consideration of other
options.

It is widely accepted (Anderson, Spiro & Anderson,
1978) that structures or schemata influence acquisition
(original learning), retention, and problem solving; and
agreement exists also as to the influence of the structures
on reception—recognizing, sensing, perceiving. There is
much evidence indicating that this is the case—that the way
a person organizes items of information or the habitual way
the person has organized similar items influences perception and recognition of potential items of information.

Bruner and Potter (1964) and Potter (1966) investigated this issue. Their data indicate that when persons are confronted with unfocused photographs and asked to identify the object in the photograph as it is gradually focused, the early hypotheses tend to interfere with later correct identification. The subjects appeared to be unwilling to change these hypotheses about the identity of the object photographed.

The unwillingness resulted in delaying the identification. Apparently, when a person encounters an ambiguous array of potential information, the tendency is to impose some structured meaning from previous experience on it, and the person is then unwilling to surrender these. These structures inhibit accurate recognition when they are in error. This is clearly a form of resistance to change which can impede learning.

This section has presented investigations which indicate the influence of previously learned structures on original learning, transfer, problem solving, and recognition (both sensation and perception). To summarize, the following principles appear to be supported by the evidence adduced:

1. Persons will impose a previously learned structure on ambiguous stimuli.
2. Humans tend to organize even unrelated material when there is a requirement to remember, and the organization helps short-term memory. This organization obviously emerges from previous learning.
3. Optimum conditions for learning exist when the structures are both logically and psychologically meaningful.
4. Structures aid problem solving.
5. Generally speaking, some previous knowledge involving at least minimal structuring is desirable, if not necessary, to recognition.

Recognition implies perceiving something relatable to previous learnings. Recognizing something new involves bringing to bear previously learned material in a new combination and fitting the new into some organizational structure, some interrelated set of already-internalized meanings.

The idea that we perceive and remember in terms of our concepts and structures operating at the moment of observation leads toward the notion that little, perhaps nothing, new can be learned. In the extreme of this idea, perception, remembering, and knowing are static and closed.

Surely such an extreme interpretation is misleading and not justified. Experiments such as Anderson and Ortony (1975) indicate that, while cognitive structures do influence sentence recall, there is an interplay between the person's cognitive structures obtaining at the time of reading the sentence and the sentence content. The sentence content has the possibility of modifying the cognitive structure. There is no evidence which suggests that this is not also true for stimulus material other than prose.

Summary

Psychological research supports the thesis that our knowledge strongly influences how we perceive new stimuli and construct new information. This research seems to support the notion of relativistic subjectivity as we presented it in chapter 1.

A culture and a social order depend in part on numbers of persons sharing concepts and structures. The shared knowledge establishes a cultural orientation and cultural sets or biases which will in part control individual perception.

Since all persons in a given culture have some similar experiences and some unique experiences, we may expect that any given individual will have some communal perceptual predispositions and some very unique perceptual predispositions. Thus, we may expect that any given social order may suffer from information distortion as well as any given individual.

CHAPTER 4

How What We Feel Distorts Information

In the preceding chapter we saw how a person's knowledge influences perceptions and information. In this chapter we will examine how a person's feeling's and other aspects of the frame of reference operate on perception as well as on information extraction and construction. I have organized these components of the frame of reference into four appropriate headings: affect, values, needs, and interests.

Affect

English and English (1958:15) define affect as "a class name for feeling, emotion, mood, temperament." Affect is difficult to separate from the other five components of the frame of reference in that it continuously interacts with all of them. Affect is involved in the acquisition and maintenance of attitudes and values. Affects are aroused in connection with our interests and needs. Psychological literature reflects no small disagreement on interrelationships between affect and a variety of other constructs. It should suffice here to note that there is affective or emotional arousal in connection with attitudes including biases, prejudices, beliefs, values, interests, and needs. Humans value those objects and contexts with and within which needs are met, and interests are exercised and expressed thereto. Affective arousal occurs during the process of meeting needs, expressing interests, and maintaining values. Affect cannot be completely divorced from our concepts and structures; we value what we know and can feel threatened when others challenge our explanations. A person who has already formed a concept about or an explanation of an event will usually affectively resist revising that concept or explanation.

Some influences of affect on sensation, perception, learning, and thinking will be mentioned in this section. While there is much evidence to support an argument that there are such influences, the evidence is beclouded by methodological and inferential problems (Schultz, 1974; Wyer, 1975). The most scientific approach would be to regard statements of such influences and relationships as hypotheses which may be supported or challenged by various findings. Psychologists are not in agreement on these issues. For example, Fishbein (1967:478) notes that attitudes, as conventionally measured, do not predict behavior very well; like Thurstone (1931), he regards attitude and affect as nearly synonymous. It would seem that in light of the above hypotheses one can show relationships between affect and the cognitive processes without being required to predict exactly what the person will do in a specific situation. While the affective arousal of two persons to an object may be roughly the same, overt responses may be very different as the two persons may have learned to behave differently to the similar feelings.

Although I include six components within the frame of reference, strict distinctions between affect, value, interest, and need are not possible. However, some useful distinctions can be made in attempts to communicate behavioral integration and wholeness rather than fragmentation. During this and the following sections the reader may well believe that one study is illustrating the impact of values while I argue that it illustrates the impact of affect. When a study has been traditionally regarded as illustrating an influence of a need, value, or interest on cognitive processes, I have tried to include it within the appropriate section.

Several points may be made which will illustrate the global influences of affect on perception and information.

1. A person given some freedom will tend to seek or approach an object, a task, or a situation for which that person has positive affect.
2. Humans will tend to avoid that for which they have negative affect.
3. The emotional state of the person partially determines what is perceived.

These tendencies continuously operate to place a person in contextual settings which provide relative continuity to personal perceptions and support personal concepts and structures.

One specific area of affect, anxiety, has been shown to have debilitating influence on cognitive processes (Sarason et al., 1960; Harleston, 1962; Ruebush, 1960; West et al., 1969), although the effects of the nature of the task and other variables such as intelligence cannot be discounted. Some anxiety also appears to have a motivating influence, while anxiety in excess is detrimental. Combs and Syngg (1959) argue that anxiety narrows perception. West et al., (1969) present evidence that high anxiety decreases one's ability to select relevant from irrelevant information. One could tentatively conclude that either high or low extremes of anxiety are associated with lower performance than are more moderate levels of anxiety. Moderate anxiety is related to motivation in that it appears to promote performance.

Affect influences the cognitive processes. Some evidence exists that affect may have specific effects on sensation and perception. Findings from a series of studies (McGinnies, 1949; Cowen and Beier, 1952; Fulkerson, 1957) indicate that "taboo" words (words which have negative affective connotation or are "socially unacceptable") are more difficult to recognize than affectively neutral words. It may be that subjects in these studies recognized the words, but were reluctant to say them. Tomkins (Tomkins and Izard, 1965) presented subjects with contrasting pictures in a stereoscope. A photograph with a smiling face was presented on one side of the stereoscope and a photo of the same person with a contemptuous face on the other. Subjects with a humanistic orientation and positive feelings about themselves and others tended to see the smiling face. Subjects with more negative feelings about themselves and others tended to see the contemptuous face.

Projection, one of the ego defense mechanisms of psychoanalytic theory, exemplifies the influence of affect on what is sensed and perceived. During the administration of Rorschach inkblots, examiners note that subjects "project" or "see" that which is consistent with their feelings and fears. The same phenomenon occurs with other projective techniques. Frequently, subjects' reports from item to item are on a related theme—a person who feels threatened reports seeing threatening people and situations. These observations and the above findings lend support to the hypothesis that affect influences sensation and perception, that we see what is consistent with our idiosyncratic frame of reference.

McGeoch and Irion (1952) and Bugelski (1956) note some consensus in psychology as to the influence of affect on learning and retention. Apparently affectively charged material is retained better than more neutral material, and pleasant material is often better retained than unpleasant topics. Dutta and Kanungo (1975) report that retention of affective material is more a function of the intensity of affect rather than the quality of the affect. Kleinsmith and Kaplan (1963; 1964) found that high arousal inhibited immediate recall of paired words, but aided long-term retention when compared to low-arousal words. Earlier, Worchel (1955) found that items associated with negative affect material are not retained as well as those associated with neutral material. Izard et al., after a series of investigations, conclude

> Pictures with different affect scale ratings evoke significantly different cognitive performance (learning rates) ... Both intensity *and* quality of affect are significant factors in altering behavior, ... The relationship or relevance of the affect-inducing stimuli (e.g., whether they are figure or ground) to concomitant or subsequent cognitive processes (e.g., learning) is of great importance in determining the influence of affect on performance. (Tomkins and Izard, 1965)

There is also evidence which indicates that problem solving is influenced by affective variables. The primary question is "What is the effect of emotional content on reasoning?"

Janis and Frick (1943) investigated the influence of subjects' attitudes on solving syllogisms. Sixteen syllogisms, eight valid and eight invalid, were presented. Syllogisms were selected with a minimum of neutral content so as to arouse agreement or disagreement. There were four categories: valid with agreement or disagreement and invalid with agreement or disagreement. Subjects were told to judge the syllogisms as to whether or not the conclusions followed logically from the premises. After judging the syllogisms, subjects were given an attitude test made up of the conclusions of the syllogisms. Subjects reported whether they agreed or disagreed with the statements. Their evidence supports the notion that people are more likely to accept invalid conclusions if they agree and are more likely to be critical of valid conclusions if they disagree. In later studies (Lefford, 1946; Frase, 1966; Kaufmann and Goldstein, 1967), support was found for this same conclusion.

Thistlewaite (1950) constructed test items so that they were nearly identical except for the variation in emotional content. College-age groups from various regions of the United States were tested. Statistical interpretation indicated less error on the neutral items than on the emotionally toned items.

In sum, considerable empirical evidence exists indicating the impact of affect on the basic processes involved in human cognition. The residues of experience which result when a person encounters an event—with resulting stimulation—is not only a function of the event and its stimulating potential, but also of the affective state of the person.

Values

By value I mean a relatively enduring sense of worth or "goodness" attributed to classes of experiences, behaviors, and beliefs. In this section I will discuss the impact of human values and valuing on how we think, sense, and perceive. In the section on affect, it was noted that values are related to affect. If we value something, affect is obviously involved. We also invest value in our concepts and structures and seek to maintain them. This consistency is another source of stability and resistance to change.

Rokeach (1967) has drawn a distinction between terminal and instrumental values. Terminal values are characterized as desirable end states of existence, and instrumental values are desired modes of behavior. Values are more general than affects or attitudes which are tied to specific objects and settings in that they constitute standards by which to judge the worth of classes of behaviors and goals. Thus, while an individual may learn hundreds and thousands of attitudes throughout a lifetime, an individual may acquire relatively few, perhaps a few dozen, values.

Postman, Bruner, and McGinnies (1948) found that subjects recognized words related to their highly prized values more rapidly than they would recognize words related to values not so highly prized. In another study, Bruner and Goodman (1947) found support for an influence of values on perception. The task for members of the experimental group of ten-year-olds was to adjust the size of a light spot by turning a knob until the spot was the same size as the subjects thought coins to be. The experimental subjects first estimated from memory the size of coins from a penny to a half dollar. The control subjects followed the same procedure, but were told to estimate the sizes of cardboard disks cut to the same sizes as the coins.

The results indicated that the coin size was overestimated significantly in comparison to the judgement of the cardboard disks. The percentage of overestimation ranged from 15 percent of overestimations of the penny to nearly 40 percent of overestimations of the quarter, with 35 percent of overestimations of the half dollar. The neutral stimuli were not subject to overestimation. Moreover youngsters from "poor homes" drastically overestimated the size of coins compared to children from "rich homes." In yet another study by Ashley, Harper, and Runyan (1951), subjects were shown a metal slug. They were told that the slug was lead, silver, white gold, or platimun. The subjects' estimations of the size of the slug were positively correlated with the "value" (or what they were told about value) and the amount of overestimation. Jenkins (1957) noted a related phenomenon.

Political values appear to be a source of distortion in cognition. Edwards (1941) noted that political orientation influenced recognition. Pecjak et al. (1970) found that religious affiliation of subjects influenced the evaluation of a relatively large number of concepts. In another study, Levine and Murphy (1943) found evidence that political values influence original learning and, later, retention of materials. Procommunist and anticommunist college students were identified. Each group read and reproduced both procommunist and anticommunistic prose passages. The procommunist students learned the anticommunist material more slowly and forgot that material more rapidly than the anticommunist students. More recent studies with more sophisticated designs such as Spiro and Sherif (1975) have failed to support such a direct selective relationship as was noted by Levine and Murphy (1943). Nonetheless, it remains that there are substantial relationships between ego involvement and retention (Spiro and Sherif, 1975).

Rokeach (1971) reports results of a series of three studies on the experimental modification of values, attitudes, and behaviors of college students. His concern was with the terminal values of freedom and equality, attitudes toward civil rights, and actual participation in civil rights activities. Through a clever procedure whereby students were caused to become aware of discrepancies between their values, attitudes and behaviors, tendencies to change in the direction of consistency were noted. Moreover these changes persisted over periods of time ranging up to twenty-one months.

In the same set of investigations, Rokeach noted the interesting result that value change typically preceded attitude change. These findings taken together suggest that attitudes (that is evaluations) of specific beliefs about things may vary or be altered only within the scope of a more general value system. That is, a person's values limit the range of specific attitudes he may hold. Furthermore, in order for major shifts in attitudes to occur—e.g., from a strong procivil-rights to a strong anticivil-rights position, changes in the corresponding values are indicated. Clearly, more research is needed to determine what are necessary and what are sufficient conditions for attitude and value change.

In general, the evidence suggests that values influence

perception, judgment, recognition, learning, and memory. It is also probable that there is a great deal of resistance to responding in ways that are inconsistent to values. There is evidence that forcing individuals to behave in ways that are inconsistent with their values will have the affect of producing motivation for change. The tendency is toward consonance between values and behavior, not dissonance. When relatively free, we will respond in ways consistent with our values. When forced to respond in ways inconsistent with our values, we experience pressure to change our values, behavior, or beliefs, or all three (Festinger, 1957; Festinger and Carlsmith, 1959; Deutsch and Collins, 1951; Rokeach, 1971).

Research in values indicates that individuals form associations more rapidly when they are congruent with their own values (Bousfield and Samborski, 1955), and are more efficient in grouping and retaining such congruent items (Mayzner and Tresselt, 1955).

Thus it appears that theory, research, and clinical experience support the notion that values play important roles in influencing cognition, along with the other factors in the frame of reference.

Needs

Several investigators indicate that a person's basic needs influence perception in part. Levine, Chein, and Murphy (1942) deprived humans of food for one, three, six, and nine hours. Subjects identified objects from pictures which were distorted through a ground glass screen. There were pictures of food, miscellaneous household articles, and meaningless figures. There was a relationship between the time of deprivation and the frequency of the identification of food objects. That is, those subjects deprived of food for longer periods tended to identify many of the pictures as photographs of food objects.

In one study already mentioned in Chapter 2 involving cats (Hernandez-Peon et al., 1956), the experimenters were able to record signals from the brains of cats. When a clicking sound was made, the neural record indicated a change in the cat's brain. A jar containing two live mice was placed before the cat. Again the clicking sound was made near the cat's ear, but the neural record in the brain indicated no change. Apparently the animal was attending so closely to the mice that the signal did not reach the brain. Similarly, these investigators found that a strong olfactory stimulus—fish odors—was sufficient in distracting the cat's attention to block off the auditory input to the brain.

Postman and Crutchfield (1952) found that needs act as a device in the selection of stimuli in a problem-solving task. Those stimuli which fit a need are attended to in preference over other potential stimuli.

McClelland and Atkinson (1948) also studied the effects of food deprivation upon responses to neutral stimuli. The investigators projected ambiguous stimuli on a screen and required the subjects to make associations to them. As the time of food deprivation increased, the number of food-related responses increased. A related effect was found by Atkinson and McClelland (1948) in the area of thematic apperception. Subjects wrote stories about eight ambiguous pictures after one, four, or sixteen hours of food deprivation. A positive relation was found between hours of deprivation and the number of food deprivation themes written by the subjects. Expressed need for food and activity for overcoming deprivation also increased with increased deprivation.

Interests

Experiments have demonstrated that young children can comprehend more material of high interest to them than they do material of low interest (Asher, 1977; Asher, Hymel, & Wigfield, 1978). Furthermore, boys learn just as much as girls if the material presented is of high interest, but boys do not learn as much as girls if the material is of low interest (Asher and Markell, 1974).

Asher (1977) indicates that the influence of interest may be attributed to either motivation or previous knowledge. It could be that interesting material helps to maintain the person's attention, so that the person makes greater effort. On the other hand, the person may learn more, or may indicate on a test that more was learned, because of previous knowledge or because of having an effective and pertinent cognitive structure prior to reading the material.

It is very difficult to isolate the influence of interests on sensation, perception, and cognition. However, the evidence for affect, value, and need noted earlier in this chapter is related to this issue in that humans are interested in those things they feel strongly about—things which they need and value. We may say that, at least indirectly, psychological evidence does exist for such an influence. One's everyday experience should provide one with some support for the notion that interests influence sensation and perception.

Blair, Jones, and Simpson (1968: 201 ff.) refer to interests as specific positive attitudes with a motivational component. They regard interests as causes of seeking behavior. Interests may be based on needs in that in response to a need an individual might be expected to become interested in activities which lead to satisfaction of that need.

Anecdotal evidence may be cited to show that when an event occurs in our immediate environment which is consistent with our interests, we may be more likely to sense and perceive it. My son Kenyon had developed by age three a consuming interest in trains. During an automobile drive, many "attention worthy" objects were available to him, but trains and train-related objects were selected especially for attention. My wife and I may not have noticed a train or track (with semaphore!) nearby, but the reader may rest assured that train-related stimuli were brought to our attention. Likewise, if Kenyon were watching television or playing with friends, he might not hear a call to dinner. How much of the latter illustration is due to selective attention and how much is attributable to other factors is a matter for conjecture.

All normal people have the ability to concentrate on those things in which they are interested, and this reduces the salience of other potential stimuli. In terms of problem solving and thinking, such channelization is necessary, for, as has been mentioned, one does not have the capacity to respond simultaneously to every potential internal and external stimulus. If such channelization were not possible, sustained and complex behaviors such as problem solving could not occur.

The total influence of interest tends to place us in situations in which we will perceive stimuli that are consistent with those interests. Interests also channel our attention in certain directions by fixing our attention on certain stimuli selected out of all the potential stimuli which constantly surround us. There is also the cumulative effect of these two. Over years of experience, what has been learned in terms of concepts, structures, and affect may serve to intensify the influence of interests on sensation, perception, and cognition.

Conclusions and Summary

Much puzzlement exists as to why people do not always act in a logical, thoughtful fashion. It is known that most persons are capable of performing logical and orderly thought upon reaching mid-adolescence. Yet, they do not do so in many instances.

Material such as that discussed in this chapter suggests explanations as to why this is the case. Emotional and valuational factors may override logic. People will not generally reveal a conclusion or act upon it if the conclusion runs counter to their attitudes or values, even if the conclusion is reached logically.

People can generally be relied upon to use all their logical skills to evaluate a conclusion about which they disagree. Great effort will be made to show error and to refute such a conclusion. On the other hand logic will not necessarily be employed against conclusions with which they agree. This important point strongly suggests that persons should be most consciously guarded in regard to significant information with which they are in agreement. The natural inclinations of people keep them guarded against information with which they are in disagreement. Conscious efforts must be made to carefully and logically examine information, arguments, and conclusions with which one is in agreement.

In the foregoing sections, the influence of the affective components of the frame of reference on cognition has been discussed. We have shown how these components serve to partially direct what stimulates humans, what evokes human responses, and what humans think about.

Psychological research generally supports the thesis that the feelings, values, needs, and interests of an individual will influence the information derived from the world. There is ample evidence that these four components of the frame of reference act as selective filters for construction and distortion.

Needless to say, the items of information which we receive from other persons have gone through a series of selective procedures. These selective procedures include:
1. The limited range of stimuli receivable by the senses.
2. The limited, select number of stimuli to which one may attend at any given moment.
3. The selective procedures of the frame of reference—both cognitive and affective.

The selective procedures of the frame of reference about

which we have written in chapters 2, 3, and 4 seem to operate by and large at a level below conscious awareness. We can become conscious of these selective processes only by studying them.

These unconscious processes operate even in the best-intentioned persons. In a person whose conscious purposes are propaganda and persuasion, we must recognize that conscious selection of information also operates. In propagandistic and persuasive communication, the communicator will consciously select and communicate only those items of information which support that person's intentions.

Thus we must take great care as we attend to information provided to us by others to note the intentions of the communicator. We know that on the unconscious level that person has distorted information. It is possible that there has been further distortion and selectivity of information on a conscious level. That is to say, the receiver of a communication must attempt to study the intention of the provider of information. We must have as much data as possible as to the communicator's frame of reference and intentions. We must be aware to the greatest extent possible what that person's needs and values are.

We must also note what the communicator desires that we do, for it is very likely that that person has presented only the information consistent with that person's desires and intentions for us.

Of course, what we have said about another person also applies to us. Just as surely as information provided by others suffers from the biases of intentions and frame of reference, so also do our own intentions and frame of reference selectively distort the information we personally gather and attempt to communicate.

CHAPTER **5**

How Groups
Distort Information

*What a person knows and believes is in principle pre-
dictable from two classical factors, his needs and his
environment, his environment being essentially his society.*
Gustav Bergmann
Ethics

*I have determined that there is no market for talking
pictures.*
Thomas Edison

The social order with its attending culture surrounds us like
a porous shield. It magnifies certain events in reality and
reduces others. It influences all attempts at information
derivation through direct partial control of perception and
through its shaping of the individual's perception as a result
of its training of individuals throughout the individual's
history.

The social group has at its disposal the two most powerful behavioral control and shaping techniques we know.
These techniques are also used by the social group to influence perception.

These two techniques are reinforcement and modeling,
or imitation. In reinforcement the group manipulates the
rewards and punishments which an individual may obtain.
If the individual behaves as the group desires, appropriate
rewards are provided to the individual. So also, if the

person perceives things in the manner in which the group desires, the individual is rewarded. If not, the individual is punished.

In imitative learning, individuals in the group model the behaviors and perceptions which are considered appropriate. This increases the probability that a single individual will behave and perceive in the same way as the group.

In the laboratory a social scientist can control and manipulate reinforcers as well as model appropriate behavior and perceptions. These behavior control techniques may be investigated separately or together. In recent years, a very astute research psychologist named Albert Bandura has combined these two behavior control techniques in the laboratory (Bandura, 1969). It is safe to say that taken together the techniques are efficient to a powerful degree.

In some of this research, Bandura and his associates have studied aggressive behavior through a combination of reinforcement and imitation. Suppose a young child views a film in which an adult (the model in this case) performs an aggressive act. The probability is very high that the child will commit an aggressive act a few minutes later if given the opportunity. This probability is increased when the film shows the adult receiving some reward. Should the child commit an aggressive act (and the probability is very high that the child will) and then receive a reward, more and more aggressive acts will be committed.

Such series of modeling and reinforcing events occur frequently outside the psychological laboratory. Each day, practically all of us have actions and perceptions modeled for us, and we are either rewarded or punished by the group to the extent that we copy appropriately. Such natural group control situations occur even for the relatively independent and high-achieving educational psychologist—as well as for a child or an adolescent—as we struggle for a modicum of freedom from control of behavior and perception by students, colleagues, one's dean and department chairman, and one's publisher, if not one's spouse and children—my children have been known to say, Daddy, you *are* weird! When I deviate, my children perceive weirdness; my students, irrelevance; my colleagues, lack of scholarship; my dean, lack of prestige in the field; my publisher, failure of communication; and my wife, the failure to understand and to be mature. Of course, it is not those descriptions which bother me, it's the predictable lack of reward which really smarts.

Bandura (1969) has discussed three ways in which imitation influences persons. The first of these is observational learning. This imitative influence occurs when a person performs a response for the first time. The learner observes someone else performing a response and copies it. This may be a new word or a new swimming stroke. This is one of the primary ways humans learn.

The second imitative influence is termed response inhibition or disinhibition. In understanding this influence we posit in the learner a reluctance to perform an act. Take an example in which two persons are shopping. If one of the persons, the model, shoplifts, this is likely to reduce the learner's reluctance or inhibition to steal. Whether the learner steals or not will depend at least partially on what happens to the model—the reinforcement in the situation. If the model is caught and arrested, the learner will be even more reluctant (inhibited) to steal. If, on the other hand, the model gets away with the object, this will disinhibit the learner, and the learner will be less reluctant to steal. Obviously, the idea of response inhibition and disinhibition has many implications for ethical and moral learning.

The third modeling influence is called response facilitation. This simply involves a person copying the behavior of another, but it is not new learning. We have all had the experience of stopping on the street to peer into a shop window, only to have a stranger stop and do the same.

These three modeling influences are important in behavioral control throughout life. We are all attuned to the behavior of others to varying degrees. Others shape our ethical and moral behaviors as well as our perceptions.

The research discussed in the remainder of this chapter indicates that the social group does in fact control perception, but the researchers do not always show how reinforcement and imitation operate in this control. Many of the investigations were designed simply to ascertain if there were any group controls on perception, and not to determine how the group effects the control. Of course the role of reinforcement is studied in several of these studies.

Group Pressure and the Control of Perception

Some of the most interesting research into how groups can control judgment and, apparently, perception has been conducted by Asch (1956). Asch's basic experimental technique involved naive subjects as well as stooges. In the 1956 study, Asch used a group of seven stooges—persons who were told to agree on the judgment of length of lines drawn on a card—to reflect that agreement to a naive subject (one who did not know that the seven stooges had been told to reflect false judgments). The group of eight persons was shown a card with a standard line and three comparison lines drawn on it, only one of which was the same length as the standard.

On the first two trials, the stooges were told by the experimenter to select and agree on the correct comparison line, but on the third trial they were told to select a longer comparison line. Thus the naive subject was confronted with the perception of a majority. The person either had to trust personal perceptions and disagree with a majority or distrust personal perception and agree with the majority.

Under these experimental conditions Asch found that 32

percent of the total responses were conforming. Of course there were individual differences, for some subjects made no error while others erred on practically all of their responses. People vary, then, in their perceptual conformance about a very tangible stimulus.

Asch also found that as the actual differences in length between the standard and the majority choice decreased, more naive subjects agreed with the majority. This would imply that persons will conform more frequently when the tangible differences between their judgment and the group's judgment are small than when they are large.

Another very important finding made by Asch and amplified by Morris and Miller (1975) and Morris, Miller & Spangenberg (1977) is the fact that the presence of another naive subject results in less conforming perceptions. It appears that the two dissenters support each other against the majority. With some social support, more naive subjects were able to maintain their individual judgments. Asch (1951) also found that the larger the number of persons in the majority group, the greater the conformity.

Asch's research used very concrete tangible stimuli. Sherif (1935) investigated the impact of groups on judgments about more ambiguous, less tangible stimuli—the apparent movement of a small dot of light in a background of darkness. When a person observes a tiny dot of light in a dark room, that light will appear to move. This is called the autokinetic effect. Sherif found that groups' estimation of the length of movement can influence the individual's estimation.

In two experiments Endler (1965; 1966) has shown how reinforcement can increase or decrease conforming perceptions. Some of the stimuli used by Endler were lengths of line similar to those used by Asch (1956). Endler's experimental treatments and results enable us to conclude that, generally speaking, if a person is reinforced for conforming, that person will conform. On the other hand, if a person is reinforced for maintaining individual perception, the person will not conform.

There is evidence that age is an important factor in conformity. One of the better experiments which examined the role of age was conducted by Costanzo and Shaw (1966) using four age groups, seven to nine years, eleven to thirteen years, fifteen to seventeen years, and nineteen to twenty-one years. These experiments used stimuli similar to Asch (1956). The least conformity was exhibited by the seven to nine year old group. The number of conforming responses was highest with the eleven to thirteen year old group. The frequency of conforming responses decreased with the other two age groups. It is intriguing to note, however, that the nineteen to twenty-one year old group conformed substantially more than the seven to nine year old group. Studies by Landsbaum and Willis (1971) and Collins and Thomas (1972) also indicate that early and middle adolescent groups conform more. In a study comparing U.S. and Brazilian children and adolescents, Sistrunk et al. (1971) did not find substantial age differences among U.S. adolescents. On the other hand their Brazilian findings were comparable to Costanzo and Shaw.

Endler (1965; 1966) found that females conformed more than males. Sex differences in conformity were also tested by Landsbaum and Willis (1971) and by Collins and Thomas (1972). These two more recent studies did not find any sex differences on conformity. It may be that in the decade 1964–1974 more people were getting away from the feminine ideal of compliance and that these studies reflect a change in the extent in which our society reinforced females for conforming.

The findings of the Costanzo and Shaw (1966) study indicate that one aspect of the socialization process is conformance. As society incorporates the young, the youths become more and more sensitive and responsive to group pressure, at least up to the first few years of adolescence. So far as I am aware, we do not have systematic experiments which follow conformance beyond early adulthood. As a matter of fact, most of the studies previously discussed were done with undergraduate college students.

Control of Behavior by the Expert and by the Group: Studies in Inhumaneness

In this section I will review some of the most unsettling findings of research in the annals of psychology. These studies show how the individual's behavior can be controlled. They show how a perceived authority as well as a social group can cause very inhumane actions.

Milgram's research (1963; 1964; 1974) shows how groups can influence behavior. Milgram's research indicates obedience and conformity to authority as well as to the group. Milgram typically brings a naive subject into the laboratory and has him/her play the role of the teacher. The experiment also involves a student who is actually an experimental stooge. The naive subject (the "teacher") is told to "shock" the student every time the student makes a mistake, though in actual fact no shock is administered. The "teacher" operates at a consol which has a meter with voltages in 15 volt increments up to 450 volts. The last part of the meter is marked as extremely dangerous. As the "student" errs, the "teacher" is told to administer shocks of higher and higher voltage. The "student" ultimately begins to scream, yell, and cry with feigned pain. Protocols of the experiments show that "teachers" find the entire operation credible. Teachers cry, protest, tremble, but many administer the maximum dosage at the continued urging of the "expert." Indeed, in Milgram's (1963) study, 65 percent of the subjects administered the highest dosage. Milgram (1964) has also found that when a group of "teachers" are used (one naive subject and several stooges acting as "teachers"), the group can increase or decrease the number of subjects who administer the higher shocks. If the group urges the naive "teacher" to administer higher voltage the "teacher" is more likely to do so. When the group urges stopping, the naive "teacher" typically stops before reaching the dangerous voltage.

Milgram has found that the distance between the "teacher" and the "student" and the "teacher" and the "expert" makes a difference in the proportion of persons who finish the experiment. If the "teacher" is removed from the view of the "student" more "teachers" finish the experiment than the cases in which the "teacher" can see the "student." Also if the authority figure is present, more persons complete the experiment than if the authority figure is absent or communicating only by telephone.

Milgram's conclusions have rather stark implications for the study of group control as well as for control of behavior by an authority figure. Results do not change when subjects (dogs) are actually shocked (Sheridan and King, 1972).

Milgram does not think that his studies indicate that people are sadists, for sadism requires that persons enjoy maltreatment of others. On the contrary, his "teachers" wept, begged to be allowed to stop, trembled, and appeared to be very anguished. They did not enjoy it. Milgram does conclude, however, that large numbers of individuals in our culture will yield to authority and group demands—even yield to pressure to do harm to others. These studies go far into understanding many of the darker episodes in the history of Western man such as the Nazi planned extermination of Jews and, lest we forget, our own attempt to exterminate American Indians. There are some interesting, ironic nuances in such episodes. Dee Brown, in *Bury My Heart at Wounded Knee*, relates how the United States

Army was destroying the Sioux in Minnesota while at the same time carrying on a moral crusade against slavery.

Milgram has attempted to ascertain whether there are any individual characteristics which are related to conformity. He has found that occupational status, sex, and age are not related. He has found, however, that education makes a difference. That is, the more education a person has, the less likely the person is to conform to the authority and to the group. This is one of the best arguments I have seen for universal education. It has also been found that people who are highly ethical do not conform in the Milgram experiment (Podd, 1972).

The Expert and Aesthetic Judgment

The research by Milgram is of course on the control of behavior and not on the control of perception. Two colleagues of mine and I (Stallings, West, and Watts, 1973) conducted research into the question of how "expert" opinion influences a person's perception and judgment of "good art." We asked subjects to respond to a number of pairs of drawn figures in terms of which were the better or more artistic of the two. Some subjects were told, after they responded to each item, what the experts' judgments were and some were not. Those who were given that information typically began to conform to expert opinion in their following responses. Subjects who had higher tolerance for ambiguous situations were most likely to conform to the judgments of experts.

A Note on Ambiguity

It seems to me that the research which I have discussed indicates clearly that group norms have a substantial effect on how we see the world. This effect shows itself even when the perceptions involve estimations of the length of a tangible drawn line. If that is the case, it should not be surprising to find that other persons influence our judgments about highly ambiguous objects or phenomena such as visual art, movement of a point of light, and the relative humaneness of an action. So many of our perceptions involve the ambiguous, the unclear, and the intangible, and so many of our perceptions and resultant information are about the very ambiguous—consider the areas of aesthetics, values, morality, qualities of persons, ethics, and theology. Sherif's principle that social pressure operates increasingly as ambiguity increases is very significant.

Important Miscellaneous Considerations in Conformity

There are several miscellaneous factors which should be mentioned which are related to social perception, group pressure, and conformity (Freedman and Fraser, 1966). The first of these is the prestige of the communicator. The general principle is that when the communicator is prestigious more persons will conform to his judgment or perception. Once a person has achieved eminence in practically any field, that person's statements about practically anything are generally well received. Famous entertainers are attended to whether they are talking about the entertainment field, how to raise children, how to govern, or what deodorant to use.

Such hero worship is almost as apparent in academic and scientific circles as it is in television advertising. The explanations of a famous scientist are weighed more heavily than the statements of an unknown. The use of a prestigious communicator is a widely used ploy in all types of persuasive and propagandistic communications. Prestige can be real or faked.

The so called "Dr. Fox effect" research (Naftulin, Ware, and Donnelly, 1973; Ware and Williams, 1975; Williams and Ware, 1976; 1977) provides some evidence that audiences can be influenced by fake credentials. In the first of this series of studies, the researchers programmed an actor to teach material about which the actor knew nothing. The actor was selected for his distinguished appearance, and his ability to speak authoritatively. He was also given fictitious but impressive credentials, including publications.

The audience consisted of fifty-five educators, psychiatrists, psychologists, and social workers. Each audience was given a questionnaire at the end of the lecture. Dr. Fox was received well by these well educated people. The majority of the audience gave Dr. Fox favorable ratings on not dwelling upon the obvious, interest in his subject, use of examples, organization of material, stimulation of thought, and putting his material across in an interesting way. To be more specific, well over 80 percent said that Dr. Fox had stimulated their thinking. One member of the audience even claimed to have read one of Dr. Fox's publications.

Such a study demonstrates the persuasive value of representing a speaker as an expert or as having prestige. In the Dr. Fox study the audience probably knew next to nothing about the presented material. Still, the effect is interesting and people frequently must make decisions about something about which they are ignorant. One would assume that a knowledgeable person would be more likely to detect propaganda or false information.

This line of thought suggests that the degree of discrepancy of the communication is an important factor. Groups and individuals are more likely to tolerate misinformation or a deviant judgment if it deviates only slightly from group norms or personal knowledge. It is likely that great deviation would not be tolerated. Thus, credulity of information decreases as deviation increases.

Another aspect of deviation is the notion that the credibility of information decreases as the deviation from the listener's frame of reference increases. That is to say, as I attend to information, I may accept that information if it is at modest variance with my values or attitudes. But, if it is at great variance, the probability is very high that I will reject the information.

Another factor related to social pressure and information distortion is the perceived power of the communicator. This factor is related to the factor of prestige of the communicator and it seems to operate in the same manner.

A fourth factor which is related both to prestige and power is the popularity of the communicator. Some experimental research suggests that, to the group in which the popularity is based, a popular person can do no wrong as perceived by the group. This research was conducted by Zillig (1928).

Zillig determined the most popular and least popular girls in a group of adolescents. Both subgroups were trained to perform several gymnastic routines. The girls were also taught errors until the skills and errors made were the same. Then Zillig had both the popular and unpopular girls perform for the group. The groups rated the unpopular girls as making substantially more errors than the popular girls. One would assume that such a judgmental effect for popularity would carry over into the communication of information. It is very likely that persons are more receptive to information provided by persons whom they like than that provided by persons not liked.

Sherif (1961) noted an effect somewhat similar to Zillig. In his famous "Robbers Cave" experiment, Sherif was able to take a number of young boys who previously did not know each other to a summer camp. In the first week, two solidified groups were formed. The two groups were constantly stereotyping themselves as well as the members of the other group. In one part of the study Sherif's subjects played a game in which representatives from each group grasped as many beans as possible. It is not surprising that individuals from the group estimated that their own representative grasped more beans than the other group's representative, since fans' behavior at sporting events provide striking evidence for this. The "Robbers Cave" study yields much information into how biases, prejudices, and stereotyping develop in a group and how the social group helps to maintain them.

Stereotypes developed in reference groups and maintained by those groups appear to exert extensive control on how people who are stereotyped are perceived. Stereotypes held about another may determine how that person's behavior is judged. Stereotypes also influence the extent to which one accepts or rejects information or opinion supplied by the stereotyped person or groups of persons. In general, we are likely to accept information from persons whom we have stereotyped positively. Conversely, we suspect information provided by those about whom we hold negative stereotypes.

Perhaps the information distortion effects for stereotyping, prestige, power, and popularity may be made more parsimonious by the introduction of the idea of person to person identification. That is, persons will more readily identify with those who are powerful or popular or who have been positively stereotyped. We "borrow" their personal attributes and judgments and take these on for ourselves. The more we identify with them, the more receptive we are to their information and their distortions.

The concepts of identification and interpersonal attraction are very much interrelated. Robinson (1977) reviewed dozens of studies in the area of interpersonal attraction. She found that people are attracted to others who are physically attractive, who are similar to them in attitudes and personality, and who are friendly, self-confident, happy, and emotionally stable.

Physical attraction seems to be especially important in the initial phases of acquaintanceship. However, first impressions are important, for they establish sets or predispositions which may influence interactions and relationships for extended periods.

Another important factor in interpersonal attraction is the pattern of attributions which are made about behavior and attributions about reality in general. Attributions are the inferences people make about explaining behavior and, in more general terms, reality. Albert and Adamopoulos (1976) indicate that discrepancies between persons in attributions about behavior cause low interpersonal attraction and interpersonal rejection. Attributional discrepancies can occur between people of different cultures and between people within the same culture.

It is likely that we identify with and are attracted to persons who share our attributions, or who indicate that they do so. Thus we are more receptive to information and ideas of persons who make statements which indicate that their attributions are congruent with ours.

Figure 5–1. Typical approaches of the person with charisma.

A. Makes statements congruent with our personal frames of reference.
B. Uses common and well-established perceptions, attitudes, ideas.
C. Deviates only slightly, if at all, from group's norms.
D. Usually represents self as a prestigious or powerful or authoritative person.
E. Usually has a number of attractive personal characteristics with which large numbers of persons can identify.
F. Usually deals with the ambiguous.

Many of the factors which I have dicussed may help us to understand the nature of the charismatic person. In

Figure 5–1, I have listed several characteristics of a person with charisma. Considering the influence of others on our perceptions, we need more research into this type of individual.

A Summative Example

In November of 1978, Congressman Leo J. Ryan and several others in his party were killed in Guyana by followers of James Jones. Jones was a charismatic religious leader who commanded blind obedience from his followers. A few hours after the murder of Ryan and his companions, Jones ordered the suicide of his followers in Guyana. Over nine hundred people died, apparently within minutes, many from self-administered poison. Those who would not comply were murdered by henchmen.

The social and psychological factors involved in these grisly events are numerous and complex. Jones was articulate, charismatic, and physically attractive. He drew the drifting and the confused. He captivated the gullible and insecure. Through his presence and power, he isolated them in Jonestown. He became father, then god, and managed their time and their information. He took their property and massaged their minds with ambiguous dreams and external threats.

Jones had established a cult, a sect, an "in group." He knew "truth" and conveyed it; and its reception fueled the group coherence. The reception fed his egomania and social presence and added more members. Jones mixed ambiguity, isolation, authority, brutality, information management, threats of world-wide disaster, and a reputation for humanitarianism, paternalism and social compliance. This recipe was the ultimate poison, if not the final one.

Asch's findings emerged in laboratories which innocuously appeared as conference rooms. Milgram's frightening research occurred in New England laboratories full of electronic dials and meters in which naive subjects anxiously begged to be excused as the "punished" actors cried. The man in the white coat, the authority figure, gently urged compliance. Sherif's Robbers Cave insights came in the forested hills of Connecticut where young boys camped and played portentous games. But in the jungle of Guyana, in the real heat and the real oppression, real people drank poison and died.

Summary

Psychological research does support the idea that others distort the information which we obtain. Of course, not all the information we obtain at any given moment is obtained in a social setting. It suffices to say, however, that much of the information we obtain is collected in a social context. We get large portions of our information through others.

Even when we obtain information in the absence of others—through direct observation and data gathering—society continues to have an effect through its teachings and other socialization procedures. It is safe to surmise that there is very little, if any, information free of social/cultural influences available to individual persons.

CHAPTER 6

The Distortions of
Language

*We see and hear and otherwise experience very largely
as we do because the language habits of our community
predispose certain choices of interpretation.*
Edward Sapir
Language and Environment

*There is nothing magical or sacred about the relation-
ships of a symbol (a word, a coin, a flag, etc.) to the
object is represents.*
H. R. Pollio
The Psychology of Symbolic Activity

So far I have discussed information distortion and construction in terms of the selectivity of sensation and perception,
in terms of the person's individual frame of reference both
cognitive and affective, and in terms of the social group.
Distortion may also result out of the nature of the communication of that information. Our major method of communication is language. In this chapter, I discuss some of the
ways in which language is involved in information construction and distortion, not only as the communication of information takes place, but also during the construction of
information. I will discuss: (1) some of the ways language
influences our notions about reality; (2) the idea that
language transforms experience; (3) some of the relation-

ships of language to thought; and (4) some of the basic distortions of language.

Relationships of Language to Reality

Modern scientists and philosophers tell us that reality is a great interconnecting series of dynamic processes. They further tell us that what appear to us as objects which are apparently separate and static are really only transient, temporary states within that interconnected process. An apparently separate object appears to us as separate and static because of restrictions of time and space, because we perceive in certain ways, and, perhaps, because our language predisposes us to conceptualize and represent that separateness and stasis.

In contrast to that dynamic processing of reality, the English language seems to be better able to emphasize the static aspects of reality. We name, label, classify, and emphasize the temporary and separate. To name an object as "paper" is to give it a permanence that somewhat masks the fact that it is a temporary appearance, temporarily existing for us in time and in space. To name it is also to highlight it as having a separate existence and to mask its interconnectness with the remainder of reality. The relativists tell us that this paper, for example, exists out of its relationships to all other things—that is it is solid because of specific temperatures and pressures. Change these and it would not be paper. It would become liquid or gaseous and thus be quite different. Again, naming emphasizes both the temporary and the fragmentary appearance of objects in reality. Of course, such a position does not imply that naming functions comprise all or even most of language functions.

But the labels of language emphasize only certain features of that object, as opposed to numerous other features or attributes. To name an object paper reflects little about the chemical and physical properties of that object. The label paper highlights the relationship of that object to the person to a greater extent than it yields a total description of the object. By this I mean that to name the object as paper is to emphasize its use as a surface to write on as well as a number of other potential uses. It is true, however, that our language about paper is not restricted to that particular label.

Language is limited not only in its lack of a one-to-one relationship with reality, but also in its ability to represent in a comprehensive way our sensations and perceptions about reality. That is, language cannot really represent visual, auditory, tactile, taste, or smell sensations.

In terms of the possibility that language exerts a great deal of control over human conceptualization of reality, the strongest position advocating such control is the Sapir-Whorf hypothesis (see Whorf, 1956; Sapir, 1958).

The Sapir-Whorf hypothesis theorizes that language exerts very strong controls over thought and that persons perceive and think about the world mainly in terms of their language. For example, the Hopi language causes the Hopi to live in a perceived reality greatly different from the Anglo-American. According to the Sapir-Whorf hypothesis, the Hopi think differently and perceive differently and these differences are due mainly to language. This language control is exerted not only through the phonemes (basic sound units) and object names, but also through the rules and patterns of the specific language.

As an example Whorf (1956:57) believed that the Hopi language contained no word, grammar form, or expression which relates to time—to past, present, or future. Certainly this would influence how they think about reality as well or how they reflect on it. Oppose this linguistic feature with English which is very time (tense) oriented. Later investigations have shown that Hopi do recognize tense.

It seems to me that the Sapir-Whorf hypothesis has some validity, but it fails to recognize the fact that humans can think in terms other than language. We now know much more about the psychology of human thought than was known several decades ago when that hypothesis was being formulated. Humans can think in images which do not seem to be linguistically bound. Of course, many of the logical strategies elucidated by Piaget (Inhelder and Piaget, 1958) which seem to predominate formal adult thought are not linguistically bound. People also use metaphors and analogies which frequently blend language and images.

These images, metaphors, analogies, and matrices may be as characteristic of thought as linguistic encoding forms are. They also may have as much of a predispositional and superimpositional effect as language. That is, they may predispose how we perceive the world in a way which is parallel to language effects.

It seems to me that it is appropriate to adopt a weakened version of the Sapir-Whorf hypothesis. Language does influence the ways in which we perceive and think about reality, but linguistic forms do not totally control perception and thought. We should recognize, however, that the characteristics and patterns of our language do predispose us to observe and interpret information in certain ways.

Language Transforms Experience

Bruner's (1964) main point is that language transforms much of our sensory-perceptual input into a format on which thought can operate. Apparently we are more efficient in mentally manipulating the linguistic transformations than manipulating the sensory perceptual input. Certainly, in those cases in which verbal communication is involved, the transformation is the focal point. We know that we can communicate the symbol, the language units; but the possibility is not great that we can communicate the sensory-perceptual input itself or the total experience itself.

The experiential transformations of language and the resulting informational distortion and construction take place on at least three levels. At the first level the nature of language may act to set up perceptual biases. For example, a person whose native language is English tends to perceive time relations as an essential feature of reality. Such a person observes the world with a tense bias, and this highlights the perceived features of reality having to do with these time relations. Of course, time accentuation is only one specific feature out of a large number of language characteristics which may cause us to perceive in a certain way.

The second level of linguistic experiential transformation takes place as the person reflects on the sensory perceptual contents themselves. The person will interpret perceptions at least partially in terms of that person's language. You may be able to appreciate this interpretative distortion by trying an experiment. Indeed, psychologists have used such experiments to try to analyze and describe the contents of conscious experience. These psychologists, especially Edward Titchener, were continuously frustrated because their subjects seemed unable to escape the limits of language to get directly to reporting the content of their sensations. They did find that language exerted a great deal of control on the analysis of sensory experience and the reporting of that sensory experience.

Try this experiment yourself. Drop a coin on a hard surface. It is better to close your eyes and concentrate as much as possible on the event. Reflect on the sensation as the coin strikes the surface. Drop it several times and think about it. Think about the many sensations which you have about the event. Now try to describe these sensations. Try as you may you will probably feel that your language is very inadequate. Your language highlighted certain aspects and, perhaps, ignored others. There is a lack of very close correspondences between language and your sensations. Try touching felt or sandpaper and the same dissonance will be noted.

These second level distortions are not limited to distorting immediate experience. People remember. They recall experiences. If we interpret and encode these experiences using language, we will recall them basically within linguistic parameters. Indeed, we probably better remember the linguistic encodings than the experiences themselves. This is the case in many experiences. Linguistic effects operate at the interpretative sensory-perceptual input point as well as on memory. When we think about and reflect upon our experience and draw upon our experience for information, our language characteristics have had their influence. This influence is summarized in Figure 6–1.

This second level of distortion was at the individual interpretative level. The third transformational distortional influence of language is at the communicative level, when we attempt to communicate information about events (reality) and our sensation to others through ordinary spoken or written language. The sounds, words, and linguistic patterns will not be up to the task of comprehensive communication of information.

Language and Thought

"Speech is the best show man puts on," said Whorf (1956:249). I disagree and vote for thought. Yet speech and thought, while not as isomorphic as Sapir and Whorf advocated, are wound up in an intricate matrix, and I doubt if psychologists will ever be able to separate the two totally.

We can be confident that language influences thought by influencing the basic sensory-perceptual input, as I have previously discussed. Language determines in part what events are attended to by the person, and it also affects how

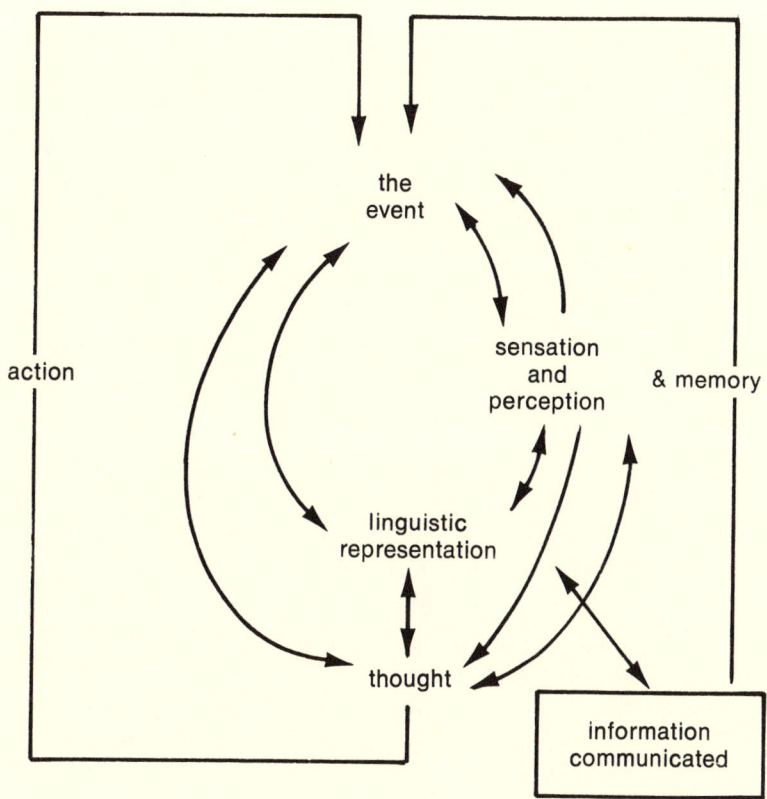

Figure 6–1. **Circular interactions among events, sensation and perception, language, thought, and action.**

the person interprets the sensation—how the experiences are encoded. We can be assured that any process which affects the information on which thought is based will affect thought itself.

Substantial portions of human thought involve classifying or categorizing reality—concept formation. We encode reality by forming concepts about reality. These concepts help us to understand reality as well to respond to it in certain patterned and predictable ways.

Most of these concepts are language based. The labels within a specific language serve as focal points or anchors for a great deal of our thinking. Each label has many mental associations attached to it as a result of our experiences. We are likely to think about the composite label plus its mental associations at a specific moment of experience. When we see a dog, for example, we would react to that specific animal in terms of the more significant mental associations we have built up around the concept of dog. We would not respond to the animal solely in terms of its own behavior at that particular moment. Our reactions occur as a result of classifying a number of experiences and resulting associations within a language category. Evidence from a number of investigations support this (Lenneberg and Roberts, 1956; Stefflre, Vales, and Morely, 1966; Brown and Lenneberg, 1954; Glucksberg and Weisberg, 1966).

As an example of labels influencing how we think about reality, consider the fact that Arabs have about 6,000 different ways of naming camels. In English our associations with a camel and with the concept camel must be limited indeed.

Up to this point, I have spoken about how labels and concepts may influence our information about reality or transform experience. We should also note that the grammatical structure of a language may have some influence on thinking. Carroll and Casagrande (1958) found that Navaho-speaking children solved a matching of objects problem differently from English-speaking Navaho children. The Navaho-speaking children matched objects following the verb form of the Navaho language whereas the English speaking Navaho children followed English grammar forms. The investigators did find, however, that additional experience easily erased the language structure effect. Still, we must recognize that there is an effect and that it can be observed experimentally. We cannot always count on the provision of additional experience to override the influence of grammatical structure on thought and resulting information.

Summary

The person's language plays an important role in information construction and distortion. Language may distort information by the fact that its words and grammatical forms highlight certain events to be perceived over others. They establish a sensory-perceptual bias. These labels and grammar structures also emphasize certain features of the sensory-perceptual material itself. Therefore, as one abstracts, transforms, and encodes experience, language emphasizes certain informational items and ignores others.

CHAPTER 7

An Instructional Strategy to Reduce Information Distortion

In previous chapters material was presented which has many implications for policy making and problem solving. Both groups and individuals make policies and solve problems, and distortion occurs in both situations. Distortions of the frame of reference and a tendency toward conforming to others are perhaps the two most important confounding factors in policy making and problem solving. It should be possible to partially reduce the impact of frames of reference and conformity by being aware of how these factors partially control our perception and thought. This awareness is most likely to happen if persons are systematic, reflective, and open. The material in this chapter is designed to help individuals be systematic, to help them promote reflection, and to help them develop and maintain openness.

It is obvious that information distortion is a concomitant part of information construction. To construct information is to slant, bias, and distort that information. Yet, we must attempt to reduce the extent of distortion as we solve problems. In this chapter, we will discuss ways that individuals and groups can become aware of distortion effects as problems are solved and as policy is made. The ideas discussed should help problem solvers become aware of distortion as they go through the several stages of problem solving. The ideas discussed here make the analysis of information distortion an integrated part of a problem-solving process. In presenting ideas on the analysis of information distortion, I have used a slight modification of Dewey's (1910) steps of problem solving to which I also alluded in chapter 1.

Problem solving occurs individually and in groups. I have attempted to outline an approach which should serve to reduce information distortion for the individual problem solver as well as for group problem solving. Problem conceptualization, information selection, solution conceptualization, and analysis of implications are labelled as steps for convenience. Within each of these four steps are several stages. Some of these stages are frame of reference considerations and some are designed to reduce conformity.

Conceptualizing the Problem

The way a problem is stated or conceptualized may exert some influence on the solution and on the pertinent information which is gathered. In figure 7-1 I have listed some essential stages for distortion analysis which should help reduce informational distortion.

The person or group should spend some time initially on examining emotion (stage 1) and preconceptions (stage 2) about the problem. Basically what is included here is the analysis of potential frame of reference distortion effects and social distortion effects. The status member, if this is group work, must typically refrain from controlling the group from the very beginning. Once these stages have been followed, the probability is higher that an unbiased definition of the problem will be developed.

Groups can aid problem solving by helping to examine the frames of reference of the individual members. Frames of reference may contrast within the group and differences may become apparent. What is desired is that the uniqueness of each person's frame of reference be fully aired and discussed.

We know that high-status persons in a group can be very

Figure 7–1.   Stages in analyzing distortion effects during problem conceptualization.

Frame of Reference
1. What are my (our) motives, biases, feelings, or prejudices about this problem?
2. What are my (our) preconceptions about this problem and the way it is stated?

Other Influences
3. If this is group work, the high status members should refrain from stating early solutions, preconceptions, or opinions.
4. List various definitions of the problem. If this is group work, encourage every member to attempt a different way of stating the problem. Encourage sharing and communicating different ideas. Let high status persons speak out last. Discourage premature evaluation.
5. Select what appears to be the best statement of the problem. What role did the high status person play in this selection?
6. Have I (we) stated or defined this problem adequately? Have we stated it only in terms of our emotions and preconceptions? Should it be stated more concretely? More abstractly?

controlling and restrictive. I personally know one very prestigious, young, brilliant person in my own field who is frequently involved in policy decision in national groups on educational research. His status is not that of a formal authority figure, but that of a highly reputed person. When he is a member of a group, everyone seems to stall for time until he speaks out, and then everyone else seems to fall into line.

Another kind of status is devised from a more formal authority. This is the kind of status which a unit head or a president holds. Either type of status can be very restrictive, depending on what the status person does and how the group reacts. All too frequently, the status figure defines the problem prior to any group meeting and simply lays it before the group at the very beginning. Group members should be sensitive to this and request that the status figure or figures refrain from this procedure. At times, of course, the most powerful members of the group do not emerge until after the group has met several times. Groups should be sensitive to the possibility of control by such emerging leaders.

Selecting Appropriate Information

During the information selection step of problem solving, the main considerations are the potential distortive effects which emerge from preconceptions about previously gathered information; from prior knowledge; from emotional bias; from group norms; from particular items of

Figure 7–2. Stages in analyzing distortion effects during information selection.

1. What information must I (we) have to solve this problem?

Frame of Reference

2. How is (are) my (our) knowledge or preconceptions influencing the information I (we) collect?
3. How are my (our) emotions, biases, values influencing the information I (we) collect?

Other Influences

4. Have we as a group formed norms, opinions, or stereotypes which influence the information selection? Which may have restricted the sources of information?
5. Discuss the possibility of the outside affiliations of the members of the group having an influence on information collected.
6. Each member of the group is encouraged to generate ideas, contribute information, or suggest new sources of information. Evaluation of these should be delayed.
7. Note what the status persons do. Have they dominated information collection? Have they dominated the selection of information sources?
8. List the information collected. Evaluate it.
9. Note any patterns of sources or restriction of sources.
10. How does the collected information fit with stage 1 above?

information, and restrictions as to the sources of information. It is suggested that the stages proposed in Figure 7–2 should help remediate distortion.

Groups potentially contain within themselves the ability to analyze the preconceptual and emotional biases of their members. The main distortion effects may emerge from (a) established or evolving group norms, (b) "over leadership" of status persons, and (c) patterning of sources of information—a group should take care that it does not restrict its sources of information. Not only should the group encourage every member to collect information, but also each member should be given ample opportunity to suggest sources of information.

Conceptualizing the Solution

During this step of problem solving, the best solution should be selected from among a number of tentative solutions. The group should generate as many of these tentative solutions as possible. It is probably best to generate these tentative solutions (stage 1) before following the other seven stages outlined in figure 7–3. It may help to keep a log of who suggested each solution and a brief statement as to what information or arguments were offered to support that solution.

Once a list of possible solutions is generated, the group should examine each of the possible solutions in terms of stages 2, 3, and 4 (individual frame of reference bias). Then the solutions should be examined in terms of group distortion effects (stages 5 and 7).

Once the best solution is selected, it should be traced back through the various steps of problem solving. Attempts should be made to examine any distortion effects from any source during any of the previous two steps. Special attention should be paid to the information and arguments which led to the final solution. Were there patterns of information sources? Did all the pertinent information

Figure 7–3. **Stages in analyzing distortion effects during conceptualizing the solution.**

1. List all solutions which seem congruent with the information gathered.

Frame of Reference

2. Examine preconceptions and biases about each solution as they emerge in the group.
3. Examine any preconceptions and biases about solutions from the very beginning.
4. Have any solutions been repressed because of emotions or prejudices?

Other Influences

5. Have any solutions been repressed as a result of group values or norms?
6. Select the best solution possible.
7. What role did status persons play in the generation of possible solutions and the selection of the best one?
8. Is there another way of stating this solution? More abstractly? More concretely?

leading to this particular solution come from one source, one member of the group, or one of the high status persons within the group? The outside affiliations of the person suggesting the solution should be examined. If conflicts of interests are noted, another solution should be generated.

In chapter 10 I will discuss the necessity and roles of two devil's advocates in every major problem-solving group. Many of the stages during these steps of problem solving could not be adequately undertaken without the aid of devil's advocates.

Analysis of Implications

The final step in problem solving is the analysis of implications. At this time, the problem solver or group of problem solvers must attempt some predictions as to who will benefit and about possible side effects.

During stage one, implications for actions, the group or individual should attempt a creative brainstorming opera-

Figure 7–4. Stages in the analysis of implications.

1. What does this solution imply for action?
2. Who will benefit from this solution? Is there any correspondence between those who benefit and the major information sources? Between those who benefit and those who posed the solution? Between those who benefit and the outside affiliations of the members of the problem-solving group?
3. Are there any possible harmful side effects of the solution?
4. Are there any possible beneficial side effects?

tion to generate as many implications as possible. It may help to state the solution in as many ways as possible. Each different restatement may call to mind different action implications.

This same brainstorming and restatement operation should help in analyzing benefits and side effects. It may be that the process of analyzing implications may result in returning to step 3 to obtain a new solution.

Summary

Problem solving and policy making processes share much in common. They are not, however, completely equivalent. Even though they are not totally equivalent, great value could accrue from the use of the strategies presented in this chapter. Admittedly the strategies presented should be of most help in group settings. On the other hand, the solitary problem solver or policy maker could create solutions or policy of a less distorted character using these strategies.

The subsequent chapters also include material which may help to alleviate distortions in problem solving and policy making which are attributable to frames of reference and conformity. In the next chapter, for example, material is included on how groups shape and control individuals. In the final chapter more material is presented which is pertinent to policy making and problem solving in government and other settings.

CHAPTER **8**

Other Forms of Remediation

What is common to all the other-directed people is that their contemporaries are the source of direction for the individual. . . . It is only the process of striving itself and the process of paying close attention to the signals from others that remain unaltered throughout life.
David Riesman
The Lonely Crowd

In order to reduce information distortion, we need to understand more about the learning and developmental mechanisms which produce distortion. In this chapter, these learning and developmental mechanisms will be discussed in terms of the psychodynamics of conformity and divergent action.

Few forms of behavior which have a learning component can be understood fully without understanding the dynamics of reinforcement embedded in human interaction. One need not be a dogmatic behavioristic psychologist to recognize the importance of reinforcement in human action. It would be unfortunate to infer that there is any basic urge or need to conform, to be dependent on others, to be independent of others, or to be a convergent or divergent thinker. The psychological literature is rife with such inferences, but it is very probable that there is no such basic need.

It is probably rank romanticism to claim that some

people are innately creative and independent and that society crushes these inborn characteristics, thereby creating conforming, uncreative drones. It is just as erroneous to posit an innate drive to conform. If the romantic views were accurate, this posited innate drive, if it were that dominant and common, would probably crush any social attempts to thwart it.

An alternative to both the romantic, Roussean point of view and its unflattering opposite is to posit that persons learn to be creative or noncreative, dependent or independent, obedient or disobedient, and divergent or convergent through more or less naturally occurring reinforcement practices and modeling effects embedded in human interaction.

Group interaction and its attendant reinforcement is so pervasive throughout the life of a person that one is usually unaware of that reinforcement. It is continuing, dynamic, frequently transparent, and typically unnoticed.

A child at birth enters a social situation. Most frequently, that situation is a family. Parents reinforce all kinds of behavior: crying, cooing, smiling, and talking. Many types of reinforcers such as food, praise, reproof, and numerous nonverbal signals are more or less systematically used. Parents smile, nod, frown, give attention to, withdraw attention, hug, pat, get angry at, look at, and look away from the child, and so on. Certain behaviors are persistently reinforced, some are not.

When the child performs as the parent wishes, these performances are positively reinforced. When the child performs in ways that the parents do not desire, the child is either punished or at least not positively reinforced.

Thus, the child learns what behaviors are acceptable and what behaviors are not acceptable. Usually, conforming and agreeing responses are reinforced and nonconforming, disagreeing responses are not; or nonconforming responses are punished. The child learns that pleasant things happen when the child agrees or conforms to the ideas and wishes of other people.

Agreement and conforming may become secondary reinforcers. A secondary reinforcer is any reinforcer which has become associated with a primary reinforcer. Such reinforcers as hugging, candy, praise, attention, and smiles are termed primary reinforcers. They increase the probability of a response occurring again. Conforming responses are reinforced by these primary reinforcers in and of themselves. If so, they are secondary reinforcers. That is, the person associates conforming or agreeing with the pleasant feelings which occurred as a result of approval by others and reinforcement by others in the past.

It may be that we not only train for conformity and agreement but that we also continually control it. Positive reinforcement may be more powerful as a behavioral control mechanism operating in the present than as a training mechanism for the control of future action. It may appear that we have trained through a set of reinforcers for conformance, when we have really only controlled through a barrage of reinforcers which continue over time. Many of the same reinforcers are used on an adult as on a child. These reinforcers are used across age spans. We only escape them when we get away from other people.

As an object lesson, think about the last time you were in a group discussion. It is likely that if you agreed with something another person said, that other person became more attentive, leaned toward you, looked at you, smiled, or nodded. If several persons shared the same idea, all of these persons became involved in the reinforcement.

Conversely, suppose two persons have reached agreement and you offer an alternative view. You will probably get quizzical looks, or others will look away from you, frown, look bored, lean away from you, and so on. You are obviously getting the reinforcement treatment. It will probably be rather disturbing to you, even aversive, but it is a very natural set of phenomena, and you may not be aware of what is causing your discomfort. It is highly likely that the other members of the group are also unaware of their reinforcement behavior.

The major point of the discussion thus far is that groups shape, through reinforcement, conforming, dependent behavior. Thus, society obtains what it unconsciously wants.

If we really desire nonconforming, creative, and independent behavior, we must become conscious of how we systematically but unconsciously shape the opposite kinds of behavior. We must make an about face in how we respond to individuals. We must begin to reinforce unique, nonconforming, unusual, and disagreeing behaviors.

We probably need not wait for a new generation to begin shaping nonconformists. We can begin the next time we go to a cocktail party or to a board meeting. It is likely that all that it takes to increase the number of disagreeing, nonconformist responses is to reinforce those kinds of responses.

It is true that awaiting a new generation—one which will not have been reinforced to the extent that agreement has become a powerful secondary reinforcer—is an exciting prospect. But we can obtain a large dose of nonconformity by changing what we reinforce now.

Basically, the primary remedial treatment is one in which we can all participate. The first technique is positive reinforcement of unusual disagreeing statements. A second necessary step is one which is, incidentally, an essential feature of effective brainstorming (Parnes, 1971); this second technique is that of deferring judgment of an idea. That is to say, one should refrain from evaluating an idea quickly.

In brainstorming, members of the group are encouraged to generate as many unusual ideas as possible. Members are told not to evaluate any ideas until all the ideas that members can generate have been communicated. Only then does the group begin to evaluate the ideas which were generated.

Such systematic delaying of evaluation runs counter to many persons' tendencies to evaluate an idea immediately. Usually, the first focus of an evaluation is the extent to which the evaluator agrees with the new idea. Barron (1968) has found that people tend toward two basic patterns; they have either a perceptual orientation or a judgmental orientation. That is, some persons have a "wait and see" attitude and want to gather more data before judging, while others are predisposed to immediate judgment. Barron has found that creative types tend toward the perceptual orientation.

Creative Reading and Listening

Not only do we need to change our habits in regard to what we reinforce and the rapidity of our judgment; we also need to teach people basic skills of critical reading and listening. The fact that intelligent people are less likely than the less intelligent to change opinions when presented with unsupported arguments (Eagly and Warren, 1976) suggests that critical evaluation is a trainable skill.

There are at least four moves which we need to encourage people to make. These moves should be made if possible before material is read or attended to. Each of these four items should be considered:

1. View every communication as propaganda.
2. Attempt to analyze the goals or intentions of the writer or speaker.
3. When possible, consider the frame of reference of the writer or speaker.
4. Be aware of the fact that the writer or speaker is not providing all relevant data on the issue. The writer has

selected certain data or ideas over others to communicate. That data and those ideas were selected which
were consistent with his intentions.

Once a person has considered these four ideas, the communication itself may be studied. It should be helpful to
consider several illogical, propagandistic devices used in
communication while one is listening or reading.

Figure 8–1. **Typical illogical devices used in arguments.**
(Adapted from Aylesworth and Reagan, [1969:69–80].
Reprinted from West and Foster [1976:160]
by permission.)

The complex question
    example: Why do educators behave so inhumanely toward
             students?
             The first question should be: Do educators behave
             inhumanely?
Appeal to the gallery
    examples: Everyone will agree . . .
             Informed people agree . . .
Glittering generality
    example: Not only is Mr. Smith a loving parent and upstand-
             ing citizen but . . .
Appeal to force
    example: You should support the findings of this committee.
             As you know, this is an important committee . . .
Arguments directed to the man
    example: Ignore Miss Smith's appeal. Her ideas are always
             controversial and . . .
Appeal based upon convention
    example: For a long time many others have done this . . .

Aylesworth and Reagan (1969) discuss six propagandistic
devices which are used frequently by communicators. Several
of these devices capitalize upon the secondary reinforcement
of agreement or conformity; they are appeal based upon convention, appeal to force, and appeal to gallery.

There is ample reason for inclusion of critical reading
and listening instruction into curricula in schools at an

early age. By the age of ten or so, children should be taught some of these forms of critical reading and listening. This could be done by selecting examples of prose and giving students practice and guidance in critical analysis.

Summary

While it is true that in our culture we tend to romanticize or idealize the creative person and the nonconformist, it may be that we actually value the more mundane, noncreative, conforming forms of behavior. It is not unusual to find as we study our values that we say we hold dear one thing while our actual values and our actual behavior show that we value an exact opposite. Some writers have referred to primary and secondary values—a primary value being what we say we value, and a secondary value being how we actually behave.

It may be that our idealization of nonconformity is a reflection of our frontier heritage. On the frontier it appeared that independence was a prerequisite for survival. Today, interdependence is a fact of existence, and the more interdependent we become, the less the independent person may be valued.

I know of no more telling analysis of today's interdependence than Riesman's *The Lonely Crowd* (1961). According to Riesman, whether people are basically inner directed, tradition directed, or other directed is a function of the characteristics of a culture and population growth or decline. Riesman views conformity or other direction as an integral part of our current cultural social situation; since in an interdependent culture, persons seemingly must be hypersensitive to the wishes and desires of others.

I hope that our culture can strike a happier balance between a modicum of conformity—necessary for interdependence in crowded space—and the encouragement of independent behavior, and between our stated valuing of nonconformity and our opposing patterns of reinforcing conformity.

Problems such as conformity and how conformity is controlled are generally thought to be applicable in some settings and not others. These problems may be seen as existing in most if not all interpersonal settings. In particular, scientists generally work in such a setting.

CHAPTER 9

Information Distortion and Construction in Science

"I always thought his great discoveries was fudge. . . ."

"Oh, I dont think much of science; and neither will you when youve lived as long with it as I have. Whats on my mind is answering the door."

> Emmy (the maid) in
> George Bernard Shaw's
> *The Doctor's Dilemma*

Most nonscientists are like Emmy and "dont think much of science," unless they think scientific information will help them "answer the door." When nonscientists do think about science, they are likely to characterize scientific information as important, dispassionate, and objective, and as opposed to "so much fudge." Scientific information is thought not to be affected by the intellectual and emotional pitfalls which influence ordinary persons. Just to use the word scientific means to many people that the information is highly significant, indisputable, dispassionate, objective, beyond reproach, free from dogma, and highly rational. Scientists themselves sometimes represent their own information this way. But, despite such faith, scientists are human and their findings are influenced by the many forms of distortion which are discussed above. The first few sections of this chapter provide an overview about these forms of distortion.

Scientists Have Frames of Reference

Obviously scientists have a great deal of training in content and methods; but, as humans, they share similar perceptual, affective, and cognitive characteristics with others. That is to say, the perceptions of scientists are selective; scientists have frames of reference which, as is the case with other persons, create degrees of selectivity and bias. Those processes and characteristics of perception discussed in chapter two also apply to scientists to no lesser or greater degree than other people.

In chapters 3 and 4, the constructive-distortive aspects of affect (including needs, attitudes, beliefs, interests, and values) and knowledge (structures and concepts) were discussed. In generating information, scientists are influenced by their affective, valuative, and cognitive characteristics and processes; scientists view the world in terms of their needs, attitudes, values, interests, concepts, and structures, just like everyone else, and their observations and findings are influenced by these factors. Therefore, one must view scientific knowledge or information in terms similar to other knowledge. Similar distortive-constructive phenomena occur across all information; intentions and selectivity operate in the generation of scientific information.

Group Distortion in Science

In chapter 5, the influence of groups on perception and judgement was discussed. Research clearly indicates that many people conform to majority opinions, perceptions, and judgements about very tangible stimuli as well as to attitudes and values. There is no reason to believe that scientists are free from these kinds of distortions.

As Bergmann (1968) has noted, the social environment is one of two predictors for what one knows and believes. The scientist participates in the values, norms, attitudes, and beliefs at the global societial level; furthermore the scientist's perceptions and judgements—knowledge and beliefs—are influenced by those values, attitudes and norms. This is the most global or general level of social distortion in science.

Much more specifity of conformity occurs at the level of the scientist's reference group—other scientists, and even more specific, the other scientists in the field and specialty. The scientists in the reference group use reinforcement procedures to induce conformity and to shape the behavior of the individuals in the group in the same manner as do other groups.

The reference group shaping of the judgement and perceptions of the scientist is very systematic as the person undergoes scientific training. Kuhn (1970) indicates that scientists undergo similar education and initiation to an extent unparalleled in other fields. During training, not only is the aspiring scientist introduced to the content of the field, but the scientist is also taught scientific methods and paradigms. An individual's completion of studies is partially, if not largely, dependent upon personal acceptance of the theories, paradigms, and procedures which are predominant or even fashionable at the time of training.

This is not to say that a degree of skepticism is not permitted. But, there is sufficient acceptance of those paradigms, theories and procedures and their content to have profound influence on the work of the newly trained scientist. In many cases there may be blind acceptance.

Nor does this social control terminate with the end of the scientist's training. Throughout one's working life after training, a scientist must face the norms of the reference group, the other people in the scientific field. A scientist's research is judged in terms of those norms, and the reputation and advancement of a scientist will be influenced by them.

Crane (1972) discusses and reviews research on the "invisible college"—a term originally applied to a group of scientists who met periodically and more or less informally in London several centuries ago to discuss problems and interests. The group ultimately became the Royal Society. Today the term is used to describe a group of scientists or other specialists who are considered the most expert by outsiders. They are the leaders of the field or specialty. The invisible college members share findings routinely and usually informally and cite each other's work almost exclusively. They are the "in group," and prestige in one's field and one's reputation in the field may be largely determined by membership in or recognition by this "in group."

A scientist typically will fit new data or information as closely as possible into previous knowledge shared with the reference group. Members of the reference group are even asked to help interpret data and determine implications of that data. This is not to say that, ideally at least, various explanations and interpretations of data are not attempted. Yet each explanation or interpretation emerges from persons within the reference or peer group, or from the conceptual and theoretical training of the scientist conducting the research. But, the conceptual and theoretical training also obviously has some base in other people.

One aspect of scientific knowledge is its public nature; ultimately, data and explanations are made public, even if the scientist is working alone, which is rare. Furthermore, the strengths of any science lie in its methods, and methods are shared among scientists. If there is a unique procedural twist it is communicated along with findings. The point of this public nature of science is that there tends to be more conformity when person's responses are public than when they are private (Tyson and Kaplowitz, 1977). This idea emerges from research such as that discussed in chapter 5. Much of the conformity observed in experiments on conformity may be due to the fact that the judgements are made public. People apparently tend to screen their perceptions in terms of their predictions about how others will react. There is little reason to believe that scientists are exempt from this tendency.

Scientific methods are so standard and so fully communicated along with findings that replication is generally forthright if not easy. As a matter of fact, any really surprising experimental findings are likely to be replicated. Thus, an investigator is likely to interpret his or her own findings as cautiously or conservatively as possible. This is not to say that scientists generally fear replication. At least, replication is a form of recognition.

Replication, however, is a consideration which does stimulate cautiousness in science. In the social sciences, data are frequently borrowed and reanalyzed when findings are unusual, suspect, controversial, or even extremely interesting (cf. Bryant & Wortman, 1978). The possibilities of replication or reanalysis not only create a degree of screening for conformity, but may also lead in the long haul toward more dispassionate and objective information.

The possibility of replication leading both to conformity to group perspectives and to objectivity may seem conflicting. But objectivity consists of being free from personal (individual) feelings or bias. The scientific enterprise is probably more efficient at ascertaining the distortive effects of individual bias than it is in determining the distortive effects of peer perspectives and global cultural perspectives. That which is objective is in a sense that which is congruent with majority perspectives or the frame of reference common to many people—in this case most of the people in a scientific specialization.

Institutional Affiliations of Scientists

It appeared to him that from afar was echoing the gallop of the four Apocalytpic horsemen, riding rough-shod over all his fellow-creatures. He saw the strong and brutal giant with the sword of War, the archer with his repulsive smile, shooting his pestilential arrows, the baldheaded miser with the scales of Famine, the hard-riding spectre with the scythe of Death. He recognized them as only divinities, familiar and terrible—which had made their presence felt by mankind. All the rest was a dream. The four horsemen were the reality. . . .

Vicente Blasco Ibanez
The Four Horsemen of the Apocalypse (1919:479)

In its most relevant form, science is a human response to Ibanez's four horsemen—the only reality, and yet divine to Ibanez. Much scientific effort emerges from how the people in a society and its institutions define and perceive war, illness, hunger, and death.

Most scientists today work in industry, governmental agencies, and universities. They are subject to the constraints inherent in the institutions with which they are affiliated. Within those institutions, most scientists hear the "gallop of the four horsemen" primarily through their dreams and hopes of profit, fame, status, and position. The institutions hear the "gallop" in terms of expansion, profit, status, and survival.

One major point of this is that scientists are not merely driven by curiosity. Their motives are similar to the motives of others, and most scientists have to work within specific institutions. In industry, at least in capitalistic countries, the primary motive is profit. Even in socialistic states, the primary motive must be much the same, but is usually couched in terms of productivity. The industrial scientist is researching toward the ultimate goal of increasing productivity and profit.

Universities generally are concerned with increasing budgets and enhancing their prestige. A scientist working in a university setting is under pressure to specialize narrowly, to seek funds within that specialization, and to publish frequently.

These pressures are not inherently harmful to science, but each pressure does influence the selection of problem areas and specific problems. These pressures reduce the freedom of the scientist. For example, the more expensive research becomes, the more the university scientist must seek external funds from private foundations and governmental agencies. Even in the university, a scientist is not free to simply choose a problem and work on it. Problem areas are usually outlined fairly specifically by granting agencies. Thus a university scientist is controlled in part by agencies external to the university. The plastic world impinges on the ivory tower.

It should be remembered that foundation and governmental personnel who make policy—select research areas to be funded—and who decide which projects to fund are subject to the same informational distortion processes as other people. The policy makers have frames of reference —biases, pressures, attitudes, values, preconceptions—just as we all do, and policy makers define and articulate the problem areas.

An overall effect of such circumstances is that social, cultural, economic, and political factors—in addition to all the forms of distortion previously discussed in this book— exert powerful controls on scientific research. The more expensive the research, the less the probability of the scientist independently selecting and researching a problem, and the more the scientist has to work within group and cultural perspectives just to obtain the necessary funds and resources. Furthermore, these controls operate throughout the stages of research which include problem selection, problem articulation, data collection, data analysis, hypotheses formulation, and solution or articulation of findings. For further discussion of some of these problems see Bergmann (1968), Nagel (1961), and Shaw (1973).

Scientists are not totally free in even the most democratic countries to hear and respond to the echo of the gallop of the Apocalyptic horsemen.

Obtrusiveness in Science:
Theoretical and Instrumental Bias

Scientific information is a joint function of many factors. These factors include the philosophical assumptions and theoretical commitments of the investigator, the operational definitions generated, the methods used and the particular instruments of observation employed in the experiment. (See Webb, et al. for a thorough discussion of obtrusiveness.) The effects of these factors on the information or findings in competent research are usually very subtle.

Observations by scientists rarely are theory-free. Frequently, of course, scientific observations make no sense whatsoever without some theoretical base. Theory suggests certain observations to be made over others, and, of course, the general pattern is to interpret observation and data in terms of one's own theoretical commitments. Good examples of interplay between theory and interpretations of observations may be found in the history of the Apollo flights to the moon (Lewis, 1974). Prior to these moon flights, several theories were adhered to by different scientists in regard to the origin of the moon. Was it separately formed from the earth? Or, did sufficient mass break from earth early in the earth's history? Scientists of different persuasions maintained their theories and interpreted the same data to support their different theories throughout most of the Apollo missions. Ultimately modifications of theory did occur, of course.

It is understandable that a scientist maintains his or her theory. After all, there will be emotional commitment to it, and few of us enjoy discarding an idea or theory we espouse or generate.

The field of North American archaeology provides another and better example of theoretical bias. One big question has been and remains as to how long humans have inhabited the western hemisphere. In the late nineteenth century it was generally thought that humans entered North America two or three thousand years B.C. One eminent expert adamantly destroyed and ridiculed all arguments for earlier habitation well into the several decades of the twentieth century (Macgowan & Hester, 1962:125ff). Maintaining the idea of recent entry was a crusade and obsession with him. There is recent evidence that humankind has inhabited the western hemisphere for at least 30,000 years (Brennan, 1973).

In any case theory influences scientific information. So does the instrumentation scientists employ. It is rare today for a scientist to do research which merely requires the recording of observations made only by the five senses; it is more likely that a scientist will have some form of instrumentation through which observations are made. A physicist may use an electron microscope; a sociologist may use a social stratification scale; a psychologist might employ a stabilimeter or an IQ test. Obviously these examples in no way exhaust instrumentation in these fields, but each instrument may exert powerful controls on observation, and the observation is always in terms of these instruments. Heisenberg's uncertainty principle in physics is an excellent statement of the problem of instrumentation; under some circumstances one cannot know whether the instruments used to measure or observe an event initiated or varied the event under investigation. Questions about opinions can initiate reflection about opinions and modify them. IQ test items may stimulate intellectual growth or change.

So-called naturalistic methods in which the scientist

merely reports observations are potentially as obtrusive as any method and may be more so; for example, a human scientist living near a colony of chimpanzees profoundly influences chimp behavior and becomes a recognized part of the chimps' world. In a movie based on a famous chimpanzee study, one sees the chimpanzee obtaining food from the observer and climbing on a hut obviously not constructed by the chimpanzees. Cultural anthropologists are quite aware of the effect of their presence on social groups being studied; they realize the profound obtrusiveness and change-inducing impact of their presence.

In psychology, Hall (1966:7–98) presents the conflicting findings related to relationships between states of deprivation and activity level of rats; these conflicts may be a result of instrumental intervention. For example, some studies indicate that activity level increases as deprivation time increases—when the activity is measured with a revolving drum. When activity is measured by other instruments such as the stabilimeter or the Dashiell checkerboard maze, the relationship either is not apparent or it shifts direction; when activity is measured with a highly sensitive stabilimeter, satiated rats are more active than deprived rats. Obviously, different kinds of activities are being measured—walking or running versus grooming responses—but the term "activity level" masks the difference. Certainly such problems are partly a result of overgeneralization, but instruments had their effect.

Scientists are generally very careful to describe their findings in terms of operational definitions—activity as measured by the revolving drum, or activity as measured by stabilimeter, in the case of research into relationships between activity level and deprivation. It is all too easy, however, to overgeneralize from experimentation and conceptually move away from the highly qualified operational definition which the researcher was using in the experiment. The labels or terms used by scientists become very important for this and other reasons.

Words and Numbers: How Findings Are Represented

Words and numbers, both spoken and written, are the two primary ways in which scientific conclusions or information are represented. Scientists attempt to describe and explain the processes and the nature of reality. From a Kantian and modern psychological point of view, of course, scientists are limited to how reality appears to them. A scientist reports those appearances of reality through numbers or language.

So, in generating information (conclusions), the scientist has abstracted from reality by at least two levels—the phenomenological-appearance level, and the language or number level. Any form of representation the scientist might use to state findings—words, numbers, formula—are forms of abstractions. Since this is the case, the characteristics, logic, and structure of the symbol system employed are superimposed over the observations. The perceptual data of the observations are fitted into the particular symbol system employed.

But, there are multiple transactions between symbol systems and scientific information along the way from data collection to representation. The symbol system may predispositionally and superimpositionally influence the observation and the data collection when a theory or a hypothesis preceeds the observation, as is the typical case. After the observation, the data are "redressed" in terms of the symbol system employed. The symbol system exerts influences through predispositions or perceptual sets which are superimposed over phenomena during observations and by controlling in part how those observations may be represented and communicated.

Other symbol systems supplementary to language and numbers are used to represent findings. Images of various sorts—graphs, charts, etc.—may be used by the scientist to represent findings or to aid that representation. These images and their characteristics become a part of the explanation and exert influence on the findings during observation, interpretation, and communication.

Scientists also use metaphors and analogies which may blend words, images, and numbers. Each metaphor or analogy may have its own unique characteristics which become superimposed over the observation. The characteristics of the metaphor or analogy are communicated along with the findings.

Scientists use two types of language, ordinary and technical, which are combined with numbers, images, metaphors, and analogies. Scientists work carefully within a technical language rife with operational definitions and terminology. Operational language is often highly socialized within a specialization group. At its best, operational or technical language is controlled and relatively precise; terms such as "social class' may imply "as measured by Warner scale"; "intelligence" may imply "as measured by the Binet scale"; "microparticle movement" may imply "as measured by an electron microscope." Each scientific specialization develops a technical language, though people outside the field may refer to the technical language as jargon, frequently contemptuously. The translation of the scientific finding from its technical base to ordinary language poses problems for many scientists, but, ordinary or technical, any symbol system may be obtrusive and distort findings partially.

Through the second level of abstraction, the representative, statements about reality become blendings of both the observation and the symbol system used to describe the observation. All too frequently, the nature of the symbolic system seems to exert excessive influence over the statement of findings.

As an example of this influence which also illustrates the interactions between language and thought as discussed in chapter 6, reflect on some attributes of language. Language is very sequential. It proceeds from step one to step two and from time one to time two. It can return to a point for correction or elaboration and then move on, but it is sequential. Language cannot comprehensively or cumulatively represent the contents of a complex idea or the nature of a complex phenomenon without proceeding sequentially. Even then, language is usually inadequate. Language emphasizes the static; it represents the static best and is practically inadequate for describing the dynamic interconnectedness of reality as posited by relativists. It plods along sequentially, predisposing us toward the apparent static aspects of reality. Language seems to arrest processes and to make reality appear static.

Thought, or at least one type of thought, is also sequential. Conscious thought proceeds in an orderly and sequential way.

The sequential attribute of language and thought may have a great deal to do with a widely accepted view that scientific explanation only involves cause-effect relationships—scientific description and classification excepted, of course.

There are scientists, and critics and consumers of science as well, who claim that the only worthwhile explanation is one which is essentially cause-effect. Causal reasoning is sequential, as is language. Allowing a language attribute and a human intellectual attribute to dominate explanatory styles and habits may be a subtle anthropomorphism—the projection of a human trait (a language attribute and an intellectual attribute) on to reality through an explanatory style or habit.

This leaves the distinct possibility of our falling into a twisted Cartesian posture—"I can conceptualize and articulate it, therefore it exists." Statements of cause have a semantic appeal and may be defined logically. However, semantic appeal and logical properties may have little to do with posited reality as it may be represented in terms other than language. In other words, language enables one to articulate questions (in this case about causation) about a posited reality which are not answerable within other symbol systems.

Scientists (even social and behavioral scientists) can replicate some events which they cannot explain in terms of causal, language statements. They can also explain in causal, language statements some events which they cannot replicate. It seems to me that this points to a possible lack of consonance among the attributes of language and thought and the nature of posited reality.

It seems: (a) that language has certain attributes among which are capabilities of articulating various concepts of cause; (b) that this articulation has a certain cognitive and semantic appeal to many scientists, many critics of science, and most consumers of science; and (c) that any posited reality may be said to have certain attributes intrinsic to it. There is no actual or logical necessity of which I am aware which assures that language attributes may make demands of any given posited reality. If one demands that a posited reality fit human linguistic/semantic attributes or cognitive and logical attributes, one may be ordering more than can be obtained. In any case, before one phenomenon is represented as a cause and another the effect, at least two factors should be considered: the routines and properties of causal reasoning and language, and the routines and properties of any given posited reality. These two types of routines and properties may not match perfectly.

If we demand that they do match or allow others to demand that they do, we may be committing the ultimate subjectivism. If they do not match, scientists should refrain from cause-effect explanations or at least recognize that such sequences appear more as a function of language-thought transaction than as a function of relationships among phenomena. Wartofsky states that "causality suffices for the rough-and-ready uses of everyday life, but is too inexact, too ambiguous, or worse, explicitly pernicious when carried over into science." (1968:291) Thus it could be that the sequential language attribute which parallels an intellectual attribute is all too frequently projected on phenomena to the detriment of explanation. The sequentiality may be distortive.

Table 9–1.   Summary of distortive-constructive effects in science.

Selection of Problem
1. Cultural, economic, social & political factors.
2. Frame of reference of investigator.
3. Frames of reference of colleagues.
4. Selection of problems which seem solvable at the time within the technology.
5. Selection of problems in terms of a theory.

Articulation of Problem
1, 2, 3, as above.
4. Articulation of problem occurs in terms of solvability and perspectives of the time and is also influenced by the technology of experimentation.
5. Problems chosen are articulated in terms of current theory.

Instrumentation
Phenomena are viewed through and in terms of the particular experimental devices used in the experiment.

Hypotheses
Developed in terms of all above.

Observation
>   Data are collected in terms of the problem, the theory,
>   the hypotheses, the individual's frame of reference, and
>   the most of the above, including operational definitions.

Recording of Observations
>   Errors, small or large, are likely to be in a direction
>   which supports the hypotheses (Rosenthal and Rosnow,
>   1969: 181–277; Rosenthal, 1978).
>
>   Many of the above factors also influence how the data
>   are recorded.

Forming Conclusions
>   Most of the factors above are involved, including instru-
>   ments, theory, and frames of reference.

Summary

In Table 9–1, many of the distortive-constructive effects
in science are summarized. This summary is organized
around seven subheadings ranging from the selection of the
problem to forming conclusions.

Throughout this chapter one theme is evident; the image
of the objective and dispassionate scientist who is free from
bias and social constraints and who is free to indulge his
only motive, that of curiosity, is questioned. Scientific information is, after all, the result of the projection of individual and collective human traits, both cognitive and
emotional, on reality. This projection occurs whether the
scientist is investigating the human mind, human social
stratification, or lunar origin.

CHAPTER **10**

Implications for Government

Archimedes once said, "Give me a place to stand and I will move the world." Today he would have pointed to our electric media and said, "I will stand on your eyes, your ears, your nerves, and your brain, and the world will move in any tempo or pattern I choose." We have leased these "places to stand" to private corporations.
Marshall McLuhan
Understanding Media: The Extension of Man

You may feel that it is a giant step from the ideas discussed in previous chapters to a chapter on implications for government. Yet, it seems to me that the single most important issue that we face in our culture today is how to increase the involvement of citizens in government. I believe that all other issues are secondary and that solutions of most of our problems—social, economic, and environmental—in the United States will be based on systematic and appropriate governmental involvement of one kind or another. I also believe that systematic participatory democracy can force our government toward more direct and more appropriate action, toward the kinds of action which we can accept. In the final analysis, everything revolves around information flow and analysis.

Few persons realize how antiquated most of our institutions are in terms of the revolutions in the media (informa-

109

tion dissemination and analysis) and in information creation. Most of the scientists and other information producers who have ever lived are alive today and are providing information at unprecedented rates.

Most of our major institutions today, and especially our government—but this also includes commercial and educational institutions—were conceptualized and organized under informational conditions prior to electronic media and massive information. The institutions were organized under the condition of very few, as well as very slow, information exchange devices such as newspapers and personal letters. It took weeks for information to be conveyed a thousand miles.

If a person were elected to represent a state, that person had to move to Washington for at least part of the year. Communication demanded it. Crucial information could be carried in that person's head to Washington, and the chances were that the information from constituents would not change for six to eight months. Information was scarce and did not tend to change rapidly. Constituents' opinions and most issues were likely to remain fairly stable for lengthy periods.

Referenda

At least technologically speaking, most governments today have access to nearly instantaneous communication. Technologically speaking, almost anyone can communicate with almost anyone else immediately; geographical distance does not preclude that communication.

Few of our institutions are established so as to synthesize and use massive information, to disseminate massive information, and to use the modern media which provide two-way interaction about information. From a purely technological view, as surely as electronic media can convey information to me, it can convey information *from* me and all other citizens. There is no technological reason why citizens could not respond daily to major issues via modern media. Computers provide the technology for the synthesis and analysis of citizen's responses.

With modern technology, governmental officials do not need to guess in order to gather information from constituents. Citizens could respond to major issues, provide information, and propose alternative actions with modern media. When governmental officials guess or estimate the wishes of constituents, or when they rely on their own information collection and synthesis devices the probability increases that these officials ultimately serve their own ends. Both the information collected and the synthesis of that information may be biased toward the personal ends of the official and not toward the needs or wishes of citizens.

The growth of the power of the executive branch of government in recent decades may be a result of its ability to restrict information flow toward the presidency and to respond to that restricted information rapidly. In the executive branch, a relatively few like-minded individuals are likely to be so organized as to collect information rapidly, synthesize it rapidly, and then respond quickly. The frame of reference of this chief executive is a pervasively selective filter employed systematically and with intent by those in the executive branch.

In contrast, the legislative branches are not composed of like-minded individuals. More conflicting information is gathered, more different frames of reference are analyzing the information, and a greater number of groups and individuals are operating with their own information gathering and synthesizing procedures. As a result, it takes the legislative branch substantially longer than the executive branch to respond unitarily.

One major reason that pressure groups are so effective

in Washington and in our state capitals is that these groups are organized to collect massive amounts of information consistent with their own interests, to synthesize it rapidly, and to communicate it to our representatives in both the legislative and executive branches of government. Our officials are then overwhelmed by data which were developed directly out of corporate or other interests. These interests may or may not be consistent with the interests of most citizens. Consider the situation. Legislators can easily feign ignorance of what people want. They are told what corporate or other interests want, and corporate interests may largely control the information which officials obtain. Since legislators do not really know the wishes of citizens, the legislators can and do respond to the information provided to them through pressure groups. Legislators can only guess at incompatibilities between the intentions of constituents and the wishes of pressure groups.

Referenda are needed on many major issues, and electronic media make this technologically feasible. Computers could provide analysis and synthesis. Perhaps a "choice box" could be installed in every home with a telephone and in every public telephone. Each time a major issue emerges, a referendum could be conducted. Governmental officials as well as citizens could have access to results. Then, not only would our representatives know our wishes, but we could be made aware of summations of our wishes as well. We could increase our knowledge about how well our representatives are responding to the wishes of people.

Needless to say, new rules might have to be developed in terms of the extent to which governmental officials would be required to use the referenda results. There might be occasions in which officials would have to behave in ways counter to the referenda results. Obviously, our constitution now provides bases for such occasions, but at least we would know the frequency of those occasions.

Some persons might have grave reservations about this development. One might say that people do not even go to polls on election day, so how can we expect this kind of involvement. I believe that people have very rational reasons for staying away from polls. Many people know that controlling the people who get in office is just as important as selecting those who serve. Simply controlling who gets into office is only an important first step. Perhaps a two-choice alternative is unmeaningful to many people. Increasing the controls over office holders and governmental officials would stimulate citizens to greater efforts of involvement.

Another criticism of referenda might be that people are too uninformed, but it is likely that being able to provide continuing information to officials would stimulate people to become more informed, so that their responses would be more reasoned and based upon information. Citizens might begin to develop systematic ways of becoming informed, and this might open our media to more rapid and complete ways of informing the public. Pressure groups would be required to inform people as well as legislatures. Governments could be required to disseminate the necessary information prior to referenda.

It may be true that referenda on important issues would have shattering, almost earth shaking, side effects. In one European country which held a referendum about entering into the European common market, the issue was so heatedly debated by so many people that families and communities were split apart. There might be detrimental side effects to referenda on major issues. I think, however, that we must learn to live with certain side effects. Perhaps we would learn to live more happily with differences of opinion and judgment. We would need rules to establish the extent to which results of referenda would be considered in policy decisions. We would also need rules to indicate the kinds of decisions that would require referenda. The national constitution already contains principles which could guide us in ignoring the outcome of some referenda. For example, if results of a referendum indicated potential for the violation of constitutional rights the referendum might have to be ignored.

For example, in Great Britain recently, a colleague of mine was reacting to this referenda notion. He suggested that if a referendum had been held at that time about expelling certain minority groups from Great Britain, the majority of the people would have voted for expulsion. This was an opinion, but it graphically suggests a need for caution even though our constitution has built-in safeguards against majority desires which might result in repression of minority groups or doing away with basic rights.

In summary, thus far I have argued that:

1. We cannot count on our governmental representatives to act in our own interests unless they know what our wishes and interests are.
2. Referenda are technologically feasible as well as desirable.
3. We would need some legislation to indicate when referenda should be conducted and the extent to which the results would be binding on the behavior of officials.
4. Referenda could help reduce the power of lobby-interest groups.
5. Referenda could stimulate citizens to become better informed.
6. A referenda system could stimulate systematic public and private provision of desired or necessary information.

Regional Citizens' Centers

Participatory democracy using modern technology would not be complete if it were limited to referenda allowing choices from alternatives. Citizens should have ready access to information about what governmental officials, elected and otherwise, and interest groups are doing. Citizens should also have a mechanism which would enable them to provide data of their own choosing to governmental officials.

In terms of access to the actions of officials, it is very difficult if not impossible to obtain either rapid or relatively complete data on elected or appointed officials. Even when citizens are provided with information, that information may be developed selectively and presented by a person, company, bureau, or interest group in such a way that the interests of the person, company, bureau, or interest group is being served. Most information currently communicated to us is communicated by some corporate entity. Each bit of information can be selected to induce predictable effects.

It should be possible with today's technology to establish regional centers at which a citizen could obtain printouts on the actions of at least the major governmental officials. The data could be developed, stored, and updated and could be relatively complete. Controls could be established so that citizens could have more confidence in that information than they have in the information which is now presented. Furthermore, it could be more complete. We now usually get fragmented and very biased information.

It is important to remember that, with today's technology, governmental officials and private corporations can rapidly obtain a great deal of information on citizens. We should make it just as easy for a citizen to get complete information rapidly on governmental officials, governmental agencies, and on lobby groups.

If we wish to increase participatory democracy, these centers should also include capabilities by which a citizen could provide information, respond to referenda in greater depth, locate sources of aid and assistance, and, in general terms, locate avenues of participation and involvement.

These centers should be located so that as many citizens as possible could have easy access to them. They also should be designed so that citizens could use them without being overwhelmed by the machinery.

Many people today fear computer technology. This is understandable in view of some of the ways this technology is being used. It is strange, however, that the negative perspectives about computers have been more widely publicized than the positive perspectives. This technology could be turned to humane purposes; it could be oriented toward liberation of peoples, rather than toward their control and surveillance.

> For over two decades there has been concern with the possible dehumanization of the individual by the computing machine. If as much attention were given to the issue of humanization of people with assistance from the machine, something valuable might ensue (Warfield, 1976: 158).

Despite citizens' fears and misgivings about computers, the fact remains that computers provide or can provide invaluable aid in conceptualization and resolution of complex modern problems. The computer has the capacity to consider more variables in more ways than the brightest of persons. As threatening as this seems to some, it is nonetheless accurate (Forrester, 1968; 1976a; 1976b).

As more information becomes available, we know more about the complexity and interrelatedness of phenomena. The data bases on many issues and problems have developed far beyond human ability to synthesize that data without assistance. We need the data, but we also need assistance in determining the composit implications of the data.

Without computerized assistance, citizens and governmental officials will continue to rely on the comfortable and well-worn panaceas, slogans, catch phrases, and over-simplifications. In chapter 1, I wrote about the human yen for the oversimplification. Citizens and officials are very vulnerable to comfortable simplifications for understandable psychological reasons. But, the more we yearn for them, the more vulnerable we are to them, the less likely we are to resolve complex problems.

Thus, as distasteful or frightening as it seems to some, employing computer systems to aid and promote democratic functioning and citizen-governmental interaction could be both liberating and efficient. Citizens and officials are equally vulnerable to simplifications. One potential of computer-aided referenda and regional citizen centers would be to help people—citizens and officials alike—interact and make decisions out of larger data bases.

The potential of referenda was made obvious with the passage of Proposition 13 in California in 1978. The outcome of this referendum seemed to influence the elections later in the year as candidates and officials responded to the taxation limits of the proposition, and there can be little doubt that the referendum influenced the autumn election rhetoric. The influence of Proposition 13 is testimony to the power and potential of referenda for participatory democracy. Proposition 13 may also be graphic evidence of the rapid responsiveness of our levels of governments to the wishes of the people, especially when those wishes are made obvious.

"Group-Think" in Policy Decisions: Distortion at High Levels

In this section the ways in which information are distorted by policy-making groups will be discussed. In this discussion I have relied heavily on work by Irving L. Janis

(1972) entitled *Victims of Groupthink*. Janis carefully analyzed four major policy decisions which resulted in national disasters:

1. Roosevelt's failure to be prepared for the invasion of Pearl Harbor
2. Truman's invasion of North Korea
3. Kennedy's Bay of Pigs invasion
4. Johnson's decision to bomb North Vietnam

Each of these decisions was made with the help of cohesive advisory groups. While many policy makers may feel that their decisions are inconsequential when compared to such national policies, many policy decisions remain vastly important, despite the fact that they are not international or national in scope. Janis' point is that each of these decisions was made by a tightly organized, cohesive group.

The president is vulnerable to the social distortion of information as a result of appointing like-minded persons to advisory and cabinet rank positions. There is likely to be some accord among these appointed advisors in the beginning or they would not have been selected. The probability is even higher that those who have been nominated and appointed will be in substantial agreement with the president. As the advisors interact over a period, they tend to become more and more in agreement and to formulate group policies, group approaches to problems, group opinions, and group judgment. They tend to become less and less able to conceptualize and entertain opinions, data, and judgments which are different from those of the group. Analyses reflect that the administrations of Roosevelt, Truman, Kennedy, and Johnson were very subject to "groupthink" (Janis, 1972).

While Janis' primary points about group distortion of judgment is aimed at U.S. presidential administrative policy decisions, he also emphasizes that other hierarchies suffer from group-think. In this section we will discuss some of the implications of Janis' and other related research for group policy-making bodies (Janis and Mann, 1977).

Group-think is defined as the solidification of judgments, attitudes, stereotypes, and opinions of a group of persons. Information is likely to be gathered from sources supportive of these judgments, attitudes, stereotypes, and opinions. The group becomes closed and rigid, maintaining its perceptual biases and restricting its analytic power. Thus, most of the forms of distortion mentioned earlier in this book are potentially in operation.

According to Janis, group-think is most likely to occur when the group is cohesive, when the group is insulated from the judgments of qualified associates, and when the leader actively promotes his own preferred solution (Janis, 1972:197). It is also likely that the longer a group remains together, the higher is the probability of group-think developing. Also, when the leader appoints all the members of the group, the probability of group-think is greater. Most executives would deny that they want a group of yes-persons around them. But protestations are not facts. Even the best-intentioned leader is unlikely to appoint persons to an advisory group whose values, norms, attitudes, and opinions are at great variance to his or her own. Such appointments of like-minded persons are likely to occur at all levels, and the selection processes of bureaucratic organizations tend to bring like minds together at the top echelons even in cases where the group members are not all directly appointed by the executive.

Lest the reader think that Janis' study of group-think is isolated and generally undemonstrated, a large number of studies discussed in chapter 5 have established that groups do tend to result in conformity and judgmental distortion. Asch (1951;1956) has conducted several studies which indicate that groups can distort the judgment of individuals. Recall that Asch's strategy typically involved using one naive subject and several experimental stooges. The subject's task was to match the length of a drawn line with one that is the same length. The stooges were told to agree that a shorter or longer line was the same as the standard. Each member of the group announced a decision in turn, and many naive subjects ultimately changed their choice to fit the group's choice. However, conformance decreased when the naive subject received support from another individual in the group.

Milgram's (1963; 1964; 1974) research also shows how groups can influence action. Milgram's research illustrates obedience and conformity to authority as well as to a group. Milgram typically brought a naive subject into the laboratory and had him/her play the role of the teacher. These experiments also involved a "student" (actually an experimental stooge). The naive subject (the "teacher") was told to shock the student every time the student made a mistake, though in actual fact no shock was administered. The "teacher" operated at a console which had a meter with voltages in 15-volt increments up to 450 volts, and the last part of the meter was marked "extremely dangerous." As the student erred, the teacher was told to administer shocks of higher and higher voltage. The student ultimately began to scream, yell, and cry with feigned pain. Protocols of the experiments show that the "teachers" found the entire operation credible, and though they cried, protested, and trembled, most administered the maximum dosage at the continued urgence of an "expert." Milgram also found that when a group of "teachers" was used (one naive subject and several stooges), the group could increase or decrease the number of subjects who administered the higher shocks. If the group urged the naive teacher to administer higher voltages, the teacher tended to do so. When the group urged stopping, the naive teacher typically stopped before reaching the "dangerous" voltages. Many other studies discussed in chapter 5 have also shown that groups can and do influence judgements and actions of individuals.

Group cohesiveness, then, can become disfunctional and can result in erroneous judgments and inhumane actions. However, I am not recommending a return to autocratic decision processes. The most cohesive group remains potentially a larger aggregate of individual frames of reference and thus has greater potential for more dispassionate decision making. An autocrat cannot escape his or her own frame of reference and may have difficulty in noting conflicting information; a group can potentially maintain a high regard for each group member's individual frame of reference and the group can structure itself to gather massive amounts of information, some of which may be in conflict with group norms. To avoid group-think, conflicting ideas must be aired and reinforced, and information must be gathered from a wide variety of sources.

Janis offers several symptoms of group-think. Groups are well into group-think when the group has illusions of invulnerability; when there is collective rationalizing; when there is a strong belief in the group's inherent morality; when there is direct pressure applied to any member who expresses strong arguments against the group's stereotypes, judgments, values, or norms; when there is a shared illusion of unanimity; and when self-appointed "mind guards"— members who choose to protect the group from disconfirming information—emerge (Janis, 1972: 197–198).

Janis believes that group-think can be reduced by the following techniques:

1. The leader should assign the role of critical evaluation to each member. Every member should be encouraged to air objections and doubts and to look for new sources of information.
2. The leader must not state his/her own judgments or preferences at the outset.

3. Several independent policy planning groups should be established, each with a different leader.
4. The group should divide into subgroups and meet separately and then later come together to work out differences.
5. Members should discuss deliberations of the group with qualified outsiders.
6. Qualified outsiders should be invited in for group deliberations.
7. One member of the group should be assigned the role of devil's advocate.
8. After the group has achieved agreement, another meeting should be held in which every member is encouraged to express any doubts and to rethink the issue.

To these preventional measures, I suggest the addition of at least two antagonists to the policy-making group. Assigning one member of the group to be the devil's advocate, as Janis suggests, might not be dramatically effective. It is not likely that the appointment of a devil's advocate from a cohesive group would promote the airing of differences since that person will tend to have been already co-opted by the group. Asch's research indicates that groups persuade a lone dissenter quickly; two dissenters have much greater potential to maintain their points of view than a single antagonist does. It may be necessary to continue to bring new devil's advocates into the group.

What I propose then is the placement of at least two antagonists, or devil's advocates, on each policy-making group. If we take the research findings seriously, one antagonist in an advisory group will be insufficient; there must be more than one so that one can support the other.

The head of any group must be forcefully made aware of conflicting judgments, opinions, or data. The head's appointees may be more concerned with what the boss wants to hear than with what the boss should hear. Thus, the appointees may select and pass on information which fits with what the head wants to hear or which is consistent with the total group opinion rather than information that *should* be brought to the attention of the group or the head. The two-antagonist system may increase the possibility that both the group and the head will receive counter data, counter judgements, and counter opinions.

I am sure that there has not been a president or even a head of a large corporation in recent years who would not vehemently declare that the last thing desired was to be surrounded by a group of yes-persons. But, to deny is not to prove. If advisors are not yes-persons in the beginning, they are likely to become yes-persons. They are also likely to participate in development of group attitudes which ultimately crystallize into group-think.

The two-antagonist system may well require that the antagonists be replaced annually or even more frequently, for groups can be very persuasive, and the antagonists may ultimately be incorporated into the group ways. The lack of antagonists may be a major factor in the notorious resistance of bureaucracies to modification. Those who rise in the bureaucracy tend to be those who fit themselves into the group patterns—those who have been socialized and initiated into the group ways. This is as true for organizations outside of government as it is for governmental organizations.

Another strategy I suggest is that the group maintain a sensitivity to its sources of information. Information source logs could be kept so that the group can note patterns of their sources of information. Active attempts should be made to gather information from different sources. Groups could be encouraged to use the problem-solving design developed in chapter 7 throughout the entire policy-making process. In that chapter a protocol was suggested for each of the several steps of group problem solving: conceptualizing the problem (six stages); information selection (ten stages); conceptualizing the solution (nine stages); and analysis of implication (four stages).

Epilogue

Perhaps the greatest tragedy of Western culture is that we have not yet systematically used modern informational technology to extend democratic functioning. Electronic media are being used to manipulate citizens, to put citizens under surveillance, and to decrease democratic involvement. It has reached the point that a recent secretary of state blatantly stated that members of congress were "meddling" in international affairs. If such perspectives about members of congress abound, surely we must do what we can to resist them. Today, you and I must force an about-face. We must immediately employ electronic media to our own free purposes, or we may find increasing encroachments on our liberty. Otherwise, our attempts at self-government may come to be seen as "meddling."

As I write this, a certain fatalism overcomes me. Many of those who read this monograph will categorize the ideas incorporated as just another unrealistic set of utopian dreams. But, the facts remain; the rapid collection, dissemination, and synthesis of information could become not a tyrannical boot that crushes us, but the most profound liberating force ever developed by humankind. The New England democratic town meeting is back within our grasp. It could work on a national basis.

References

Albert, R. D., and Adamopoulos, J. An attributional approach to culture learning: the culture assimilator. *Topics in Culture Learning*, 1976, *4*, 53–60.

Anderson, R. C., and Ortony, A. On putting apples into bottles—a problem of polysemy. *Cognitive Psychology*, 1975, *7*, 167–80.

Anderson, R. C., Reynolds, R. E., Schallert, D. L., and Goetz, E. T. Frameworks for comprehending discourse. *American Educational Research Journal*, 1977, *14*, 367–81.

Anderson, R. C., Spiro, R. J., and Anderson, M. C. Schemata as scaffolding for representation of information in connected discourse. *American Educational Research Journal*, 1978, *15*, 433–40.

Asch, S. E. Effects of group pressure upon the modification and distortion of judgments. In H. Guetzkow (ed.) *Groups, Leadership and Men; Research in Human Relations*. Pittsburg: Carnegie Press, 1951, Pp. 177–90.

Asch, S. E. Studies of independence and conformity: 1. A minority of one against a unanimous majority. *Psychological Monographs*, 1956, *70*, No. 9.

Asher, S. R. Sex differences in reading achievement. *Reading Education Report #2, Center for the Study of Reading*. University of Illinois, Urbana-Champaign, 1977.

Asher, S. R., Hymel, S., and Wigfield, A. Influence of

topic interest on children's reading comprehension. *Journal of Reading Behavior*, 1978, *10*, 35–47.

Asher, S. R., and Markell, R. A. Sex differences in comprehension of high- and low-interest reading material. *Journal of Educational Psychology*, 1974, *65*, 680–87.

Ashley, W. R., Harper, R. S., and Runyon, D. L. The perceived size of coins in normal and hypnotically induced economic states. *American Journal of Psychology*, 1951, *4*, 564–72.

Atkinson, J. W., and McClelland, D. C. The projective expression of needs II: The effect of different intensities of the hunger drive on thematic apperception. *Journal of Experimental Psychology*, 1948, *38*, 643–58.

Ausubel, D. P. The use of advance organizers in the learning and retention of meaningful verbal material. *Journal of Educational Psychology*, 1960, *51*, 267–72.

Ausubel, D. P. *Educational Psychology: A Cognitive View.* New York: Holt, Rinehart Winston, 1968.

Ausubel, D. P., and Fitzgerald, D. Organizer, general background, and antecedent learning variables in sequential verbal learning. *Journal of Educational Psychology*, 1962, *53*, 243–49.

Ausubel, D. P., and Fitzgerald, D. The role of discriminability in meaningful verbal learning and retention. *Journal of Educational Psychology*, 1961, *52*, 266–74.

Aylesworth, T. G., and Reagan, G. M. *Teaching for Thinking.* Garden City, N.Y.: Doubleday, 1969.

Bagby, J. W. A cross-cultural study of perceptual predominance in binocular rivalry. *Journal of Abnormal and Social Psychology*, 1957, *54*, 331–34.

Bandura, A. *Principles of Behavior Modification.* New York: Holt Rinehart and Winston, 1969.

Barron, F. *Creativity and Personal Freedom.* Princeton, N.J.: D. Van Nostrand, 1968.

Bartlett, F. C. *Remembering.* Cambridge, England: Cambridge University Press, 1932.

Bergmann, G. Ideology. *Ethics,* 1951, *61,* 205–18.

Bergmann, G. Ideology. In *Readings in the Philosophy of Social Science,* M. Brodbeck (ed.). New York: Macmillan, 1968.

Blair, G. M., Jones, R. S., and Simpson, J. R. *Educational Psychology,* 3rd ed. New York: Macmillan, 1968.

Bousfield, W. A. The occurrence of clustering in the recall of randomly organized associates. *Journal of General Psychology,* 1953, *49,* 229–40.

Bousfield, W. A., and Samborski, G. The relationship between strength of values and the meaningfulness of value words. *Journal of Personality,* 1955, *23,* 375–80.

Boyd, B. Talkies' golden anniversary. *Flighttime,* Oct. 1977.

Brennan, L. A. *Beginner's Guide to Archaeology,* New York: Dell, 1973.

Brown, R. W., and Lenneberg, E. H. A study in language and cognition. *Journal of Abnormal and Social Psychology,* 1954, *49,* 454–62.

Bruner, J. S. The course of cognitive growth. *American Psychologist,* 1964, *19,* 1–15.

Bruner, J. S., and Goodman, C. D. Value and need as organizing factors in perception. *Journal of Abnormal and Social Psychology,* 1947, *42,* 33–44.

Bruner, J. S., and Minturn, A. L. Perceptual identification and perceptual organization. *Journal of General Psychology,* 1955, *53,* 21–28.

Bruner, J. S., and Olver, R. R. Development of equivalence transformation in children. *Monograph of the Society for Research in Child Development,* 1963, *28,* (whole No. 86), 125–41.

Bruner, J. S., and Potter, M.C. Interference in visual recognition. *Science,* 1964, *144,* 424–25.

Bryant, F. B., and Wortman, P. M. Secondary analysis: the case for data archives. *American Psychologist*, 1978, *33*, 381–87.

Bugelski, B. R. *The Psychology of Learning*. New York: Holt, Rinehart, and Winston, 1956.

Bugelski, B. R., and Alampay, D. A. The role of frequency in developing perceptual sets. *Canadian Journal of Psychology*, 1961, *15*, 205–11.

Campbell, V., and Freeman, J. Some functions of experimentally induced language in perceptual learning. *Perceptual and Motor Skills*, 1955, *5*, 71–79.

Cantril, H. *The Why of Man's Experience*. New York: Macmillan, 1950.

Carmichael, L., Hogan, H. F., and Walter, A. A. An experimental study of the effect of language on the reproduction of visually perceived form. *Journal of Experimental Psychology*, 1932, *15*, 73–86.

Carroll, J. B. *Language and Thought*. Englewood Cliffs, N.J.: Prentice-Hall, 1964.

Carroll, J. B., and Casagrande, J. B. The function of language classifications in behavior. In *Readings in Social Psychology*, 3rd ed., Eleanor E. Maccoby, T. M. Newcomb, and E. L. Hartley (eds.). New York: Holt, Rinehart and Winston, 1958.

Collins, J. K., and Thomas, N. T. Age and susceptibility to same-sex peer pressure. *British Journal of Educational Psychology*, 1972, *42*, 83–85.

Combs, A., and Snygg, D. L. *Individual Behavior*, revised ed. New York: Harper and Row, 1959.

Costanzo, P. R., and Shaw, M. E. Conformity as a function of age level. *Child Development*, 1966, *37*, 967–75.

Cowan, E. L., and Beier, E. G. A further study of threat expecting variables in perception. *American Psychologist*, 1952, *7*, 320–21.

Crane, Diana. *Invisible Colleges*. Chicago: University of Chicago Press, 1972.

Deutsch, M., and Collins, M. E. *Interracial Housing: A Psychological Evaluation of a Social Experiment.* Minneapolis University of Minnesota Press, 1951.

Dewey, J. *How We Think.* New York: D. C. Heath, 1910.

Dutta, S., and Kanungo, R. N. *Affect and Memory: A Reformation.* Oxford, Pergamon, 1975.

Eagly, A. H., and Warren, R. Intelligence, comprehension, and opinion change. *Journal of Personality,* 1976, *44,* 226–42.

Edwards, A. L. Political frames of reference as a factor in influencing perception. *Journal of Abnormal and Social Psychology,* 1941, *36,* 34–50.

Elliot, T. S. *The Rock.* New York: Harcourt Brace, 1934.

Endler, N. S. The effects of verbal reinforcement on conformity and deviant behavior. *Journal of Social Psychology,* 1965, *66,* 147–54.

Endler, N. S. Conformity as a function of different reinforcement schedules, *Journal of Personality and Social Psychology,* 1966, *4,* 175–80.

English, H. B., and English, A. C. *A Comprehensive Dictionary of Psychological and Psychoanalytical Terms.* New York: David McKay, 1958.

Festinger, L. *A Theory of Cognitive Dissonance.* Evanston, Ill.: Row, Peterson, 1957.

Festinger, L., and Carlsmith, J. M. Cognitive consequences of forced compliance. *Journal of Abnormal and Social Psychology,* 1959, *58,* 203–10.

Fishbein, M. (ed.). *Readings in Attitude Theory and Measurement.* New York: John Wiley and Sons, 1967.

Flavell, J. H. *Cognitive Development.* Englewood Cliffs, N.J.: Prentice-Hall, 1977.

Forrester, J. W. Business structure, economic cycles, and national policy. *Futures,* June 1976a, 195–214.

Forrester, J. W. Moving into the 21st century: dilemmas and strategies for American higher education. *Liberal Education,* May 1976b, 158–76.

Forrester, J. W. *Principles of Systems*. Cambridge, Mass.: Wright-Allen Press, 1968.

Frase, L. T. Validity judgments in relation to two sets of terms. *Journal of Educational Psychology,* 1966, *57,* 239–45.

Freedman, J. L. and Fraser, S. C. Compliance without pressure: the foot-in-the-door technique. *Journal of Personality and Social Psychology,* 1966, *4,* 195–202.

Fulkerson, W. The interaction of frequency, emotional tone, and set in visual recognition. *Journal of Experimental Psychology,* 1957, *54,* 188–94.

Gaydos, E. J. Intersensory transfer in the discrimination of form. *American Journal of Psychology,* 1956, *11,* 107–10.

Gibson, J. J. *The Senses Considered as Perceptual Systems*. Boston: Houghton Mifflin, 1966.

Glucksberg, S., and Weisberg, R. W. Verbal behavior and problem solving: Some effects of labeling in a functional fixedness problem. *Journal of Experimental Psychology,* 1966, *71,* 659–64.

Hall, John F. *The Psychology of Learning*. New York: J. P. Lippincott, 1966.

Harleston, B. W. Test anxiety and performance in problem-solving situations. *Journal of Personality,* 1962, *30,* 557–73.

Haselrud, G. M. Transfer from context by sub-threshold summation. *Journal of Educational Psychology,* 1959, *50,* 254–58.

Hebb, D. O. *The Organization of Behavior*. New York: John Wiley and Sons, 1949.

Hernandez-Peon, R., Scherrer, H., and Jouvet, M. Modification of electric activity in cochlear nucleus during "attention" in unanesthetized cats. *Science,* 1956, *23,* 331–32.

Hilgard, E. R., Edgren, R. D., and Irvine, R. P. Errors in

transfer following learning with understanding: Further studies with Katona's card trick experiments. *Journal of Experimental Psychology,* 1954, *47,* 457–64.

Hilgard, E. R., Irvine, R. P., and Whipple, J. E. Rote memorization, understanding, and transfer: An extension of Katona's card trick experiments. *Journal of Experimental Psychology,* 1953, *46,* 288–92.

Ibanez, Vincente B. *The Four Horsemen of the Apocalypse.* New York: Dutton, 1919.

Immergluck, L. The role of set in perceptual judgment. *Journal of Psychology,* 1952, *34,* 181–89.

Inhelder, B., and Piaget, J. *The Growth of Logical Thinking from Childhood to Adolescence.* New York: Basic Books, 1958.

Ittelson, W. H., and Cantril, H. *Perception: A Transactional Approach.* Garden City, N.Y.: Doubleday, 1954.

Janis, I. L. *Victims of Groupthink.* Boston: Houghton Mifflin, 1972.

Janis, V., and Frick, F. The relationship between attitudes toward conclusions and errors in judging validity of syllogisms. *Journal of Experimental Psychology,* 1943, *33,* 73–77.

Janis, I. L. and Mann, L. *Decision Making.* New York: Macmillan, 1977.

Jenkins, J. J., and Russell, W. A. Associative clustering during recall. *Journal of Abnormal and Social Psychology,* 1952, *47,* 818–21.

Jenkins, N. Affective processes in perception. *Psychological Bulletin,* 1957, *54,* 100–27.

Judd, C. H. Practice and its effects on the perception of illusions. *Psychological Review,* 1902, *9,* 27–39.

Judson, A. J., Cofer, C. N., and Gelfand, S. Reasoning as an associative process II: Direction in problem solving as a function of prior reinforcement of relevant responses. *Psychological Reports,* 1956, *2,* 501–7.

Katona, G. *Organizing and Memorizing.* New York: Columbia University Press, 1940.

Katz, P. Effects of labels on children's perception and discrimination learning. *Journal of Educational Psychology,* 1963, *66,* 423–28.

Kaufmann, H., and Goldstein, S. The effects of emotional value of conclusion upon distortion in syllogistic reasoning. *Psychonomic Science,* 1967, *7,*(10), 367–68.

Kleinsmith, L. J., and Kaplan, S. Interaction of arousal and recall interval in nonsense syllable paired-associate learning. *Journal of Experimental Psychology,* 1964, *67,* 124–16.

Kleinsmith, L. J., and Kaplan, S. Paired associate learning as a function of arousal and interpolated interval. *Journal of Experimental Psychology,* 1963, *65,* 190–93.

Kuhn, T. S. *The Structure of Scientific Revolutions,* 2d ed. Chicago: University of Chicago Press, 1970.

Kurtz, K., and Kooland, C. The effects of verbalization during observation of stimulus objects upon accuracy of recognition and recall. *Journal of Experimental Psychology,* 1953, *45,* 157–64.

Landsbaum, J. B., and Willis, R. H. Conformity in early and late adolescence. *Developmental Psychology,* 1971, *4,* 334–37.

Langer, S. K. *Philosophy in a New Key.* New York: Mentor, 1951.

Lefford, A. The influence of emotional subject matter on logical reasoning. *Journal of General Psychology,* 1946, *34,* 127–51.

Lenneberg, E. H., and Roberts, J. M. *The Language of Experience: A study in Methodology.* Memoir 18, Indiana University publication in Anthropology and Linguistics, Bloomington, Indiana, 1956.

Levine, J. M., and Murphy, G. The learning and forgetting of controversial material. *Journal of Abnormal and Social Psychology,* 1943, *38,* 507–17.

Levine, R., Chein, I., and Murphy, G. The relation of the intensity of a need to the amount of perceptual distortion: A preliminary report. *Journal of Psychology,* 1942, *13,* 283–93.

Lewis, R. S. *The Voyages of Apollo.* New York: New York Times Book Co., 1974.

McClelland, D. C. and Atkinson, J. W. The projective expression of needs I: The effect of different intensities of the hunger drive on perception. *Journal of Psychology,* 1948, *25,* 205–22.

McGeoch, J. A., and Irion, A. L. *The Psychology of Human Learning,* 2d ed. New York: Longmans, 1952.

McGinnies, E. Emotionality and perceptional defense. *Psychological Review,* 1949, *56,* 244–51.

McLuhan, M. *Understanding Media: The Extensions of Man.* New York: McGraw Hill, 1965.

Macgowan, K. and Hester, J. A. *Early Man in the New World.* Garden City, N.Y.: Doubleday, 1962.

Maier, N. R. F. Reasoning in humans I: On direction. *Journal of Comparative Psychology,* 1930, *10,* 115–43.

Mandler, G. Organization and memory. In K. W. Spence and J. T. Spence (eds.) *The Psychology of Learning and Motivation.* New York: Academic Press, 1966.

Mayzner, M. S., Jr., and Tresselt, M. E. Concept span as a composite function of personal values, anxiety and rigidity. *Journal of Personality,* 1955, *24,* 20–33.

Meehl, P. E. *Clinical versus Statistical Prediction. A Theoretical Analysis and a Review of the Evidence.* Minneapolis: University of Minnesota Press, 1954.

Merrill, M. D., and Stolurow, L. M. Hierarchical preview versus problem oriented review in learning an imaginary science. *American Educational Research Journal,* 1966, *3,* 251–62.

Milgram, S. A behavioral study of obedience. *Journal of Abnormal and Social Psychology,* 1963, *67,* 371–78.

Milgram, S. Group pressure and action against a person,

Journal of Abnormal and Social Psychology, 1964, *69,* 137–43.

Milgram, S. *Obedience to Authority.* New York: Harper & Row, 1974.

Miller, G. A. The magical number seven plus or minus two: Some limits on our capacity for processing information. *Psychological Review,* 1956, *63,* 81–96.

Morris, W. M., and Miller, R. S. The effects of consensus-breaking and consensus-preempting partners on reduction of conformity. *Journal of Experimental Social Psychology,* 1975, *11,* 215–23.

Morris, W. N., Miller, R. S., and Spangenberg, S. The effects of dissenter position and task difficulty on conformity and response conflict. *Journal of Personality,* 1977, *45,* 251–66.

Murray, H. A. The effect of fear upon the estimates of the maliciousness of other personalities. *Journal of Social Psychology,* 1944, *4,* 310–29.

Naftulin, D. H., Ware, J. E., and Donnelly, F. A. The Doctor Fox lecture: A paradigm of educational seduction. *Journal of Medical Education,* 1973, *48,* 630–35.

Nagel, E. *The Structure of Science.* New York: Harcourt, Brace, and World, 1961.

Neisser, U. *Cognitive Psychology.* New York: Appleton-Century-Crofts, 1967.

Olver, R. R., and Hornsby, J. R. On equivalence. In J. S. Bruner, et al., *Studies in Cognitive Growth.* New York: John Wiley and Sons, 1966.

Overing, R. L. R., and Travers, R. M. W. Effect upon transfer of variation in training conditions. *Journal of Educational Psychology,* 1966, *57,* 179–88.

Parnes, S. J. Can creativity be increased? In *Training Creative Thinking,* G. A. Davis and J. A. Scott, eds. New York: Holt, Rinehart and Winston, 1971.

Pecjak, V., Musek, J., and Tatjana, J. The influence of

group affiliations on the evaluative meanings of critical concepts. *International Journal of Symbology,* 1970, *1,* (3), 11–16.

Piaget, J., and Inhelder, B. *The Psychology of the Child.* New York: Basic Books, 1969.

Podd, M. H. Ego identity, status and morality. *Developmental Psychology,* 1972, *6,* 497–507.

Pollio, H. R. *The Psychology of Symbolic Activity.* Reading, Mass.: Addison-Wesley, 1974.

Postman, L. Learned principles of organization in memory. *Psychological Monographs,* 1954, *68,* (Whole No. 374).

Postman, L., Bruner, J., and McGinnies, E. Personal values as selective factors in perception. *Journal of Abnormal and Social Psychology,* 1948, *43,* 142–54.

Postman, L., and Crutchfield, R. S. The interaction of need, set and stimulus structure in a cognitive task. *American Journal of Psychology,* 1952, *65,* 196–217.

Potter, M. C. On perceptual recognition. In J. S. Bruner et al., *Studies in Cognitive Growth.* New York: John Wiley and Sons, 1966.

Remmling, G. W. *Road to Suspicion.* New York: Appleton-Century-Crofts, 1967.

Reynolds, J. H. Cognitive transfer in verbal learning. *Journal of Educational Psychology,* 1966, *57,* 382–88.

Riesman, D. *The Lonely Crowd.* New Haven, Conn.: Yale University Press, 1961.

Robinson, Debra. Interpersonal attraction: a review of the research literature. Unpublished masters thesis, University of Illinois, Urbana, Illinois, 1977.

Rokeach, M. *Beliefs, Attitudes and Values: A Theory of Organization and Change.* San Francisco: Jossey-Bass, 1968.

Rokeach, M. Long-range experimental modification of values, attitudes and behavior. *American Psychologist,* 1971, *26,* 453–59.

Rosenthal, R. How often are our numbers wrong? *American Psychologist,* 1978, *33,* 1005–8.

Rosenthal, R., and Rosnow, R. L. (eds.). *Antifact in Behavioral Research,* New York: Academic Press, 1969.

Ruebush, B. K. Interfering and facilitating effects of test anxiety. *Journal of Abnormal and Social Psychology,* 1960, *60,* 205–12.

Sapir, E. Language and environment. In *Selected Writings of Edward Sapir in Language, Culture and Personality,* D. G. Mandelbaum, ed. Berkeley: University of California Press, 1958. Pp. 89–103.

Sarason, S. B., Davidson, K. S., Lighthall, F. F., Waite, R. R., and Ruebush, B. K. *Anxiety in Elementary School Children: A Report of Research.* New York: John Wiley and Sons, 1960.

Saugstad, P. Problem-solving as dependent upon availability of functions. *British Journal of Psychology,* 1955, *46,* 191–98.

Schultz, C. B. Information seeking following the confirmation or contradiction of beliefs. *Journal of Educational Psychology,* 1974, *66,* 903–10.

Shaw, B. The sociology of knowledge and the curriculum. *British Journal of Educational Studies,* 1973, *21,* 277–87.

Shaw, George B. The doctor's dilemma. From *Bernard Shaw, Complete Plays with Prefaces,* Vol. 1. New York: Dodd, Mead & Company, 1962.

Sheridan, C. L., and King, R. C. Obedience to authority with an authentic victim. Proceedings, 80th Annual Convention, American Psychological Association, 1972, 165–66.

Sherif, M. A study of some social factors in perception. *Archives of Psychology,* 1935, *27,* No. 187.

Sherif, M. *Intergroup Conflict and Cooperation: The Rob-*

bers Cave Experiment, Norman: University of Oklahoma Institute of Group Relations, 1961.

Siipola, E. M. A group study of some effects of preparatory set. *Psychological Monographs,* 1935, *46,* (Whole No. 210), 27–38.

Sistrunk, F., Clement, D. E., and Guenther, Z. C. Developmental comparisons of conformity across two cultures. *Child Development,* 1971, *42,* 1175–85.

Spiro, R. J., and Sherif, C. W. Consistency and relativity in selective recall with differing ego-involvement. *British Journal of Social and Clinical Psychology,* 1975, *14,* 351–61.

Stallings, W. M., West, C. K., and Watts, G. The effects of feedback and selected personality variables on aesthetic judgment. *Studies in Art Education,* 1973, *15*(1), 28–33.

Stefflre, V., Vales, V. C., and Morley, L. Language and cognition in Yucatan: A cross-cultural replication. *Journal of Personality and Social Psychology,* 1966, *4,* 112–15.

Thistlewaite, D. Attitude and structure as factors in the distortion of reasoning. *Journal of Abnormal and Social Psychology,* 1950, *45,* 442–58.

Thurstone, L. L. The measurement of social attitudes. *Journal of Abnormal and Social Psychology,* 1931, *26,* 249–69.

Tomkins, S. S., and Izard, C. E. *Affect, Cognition and Personality.* New York: Springer, 1965.

Tyson, H. L., and Kaplowitz, S. A. Attitudinal conformity and anonymity. *Public Opinion Quarterly,* 1977, *41,* 226–34.

U.S. News & World Report, Uncle Sam's computer has got you. April 3, 1978, pp. 44–48.

Ware, J. E., and Williams, R. G. The Dr. Fox effect: A

study of lecturer effectiveness and ratings of instruction. *Journal of Medical Education*, 1975, *50*, 149–56.

Warfield, J. N. *Social Systems: Planning, Policy, and Complexity*. New York: John Wiley and Sons, 1976.

Wartofsky, M. W. *Conceptual Foundations of Scientific Thought*. New York: Macmillan, 1968.

Webb, E. J., Campbell, D. T., Schwartz, R. D., and Sechrist, L. *Unobtrusive Measures: Nonreactive Research in the Social Sciences*. Chicago: Rand McNally, 1966.

West, C. K. Theoretical and instrumental intervention or the "medium is the message." *Perceptual and Motor Skills*, 1967, *24*, 753–54.

West, C. K. and Foster, S. F. *The Psychology of Learning and Instruction in Education*. Belmont, Ca.: Wadsworth, 1976.

West, C. K., Lee, J. F., and Anderson, T. H. The influence of test anxiety on the selection of relevant from irrelevant information. *Journal of Educational Research*, 1969, *63*(2), 51–52.

Whitehead, A. N. *Adventures of Ideas*. New York: Macmillan, 1933.

Whorf, B. L. *Language, Thought, and Reality*, J. B. Carval, ed. New York: John Wiley and Sons, 1956.

Williams, R. G., and Ware, J. E. Validity of student ratings of instruction under different incentive conditions: a further study of the Dr. Fox effect. *Journal of Educational Psychology*, 1976, *68*, 48–56.

Williams, R. G., and Ware, J. E. An extended visit with Dr. Fox: validity of student satisfaction with instruction ratings after repeated exposures to a lecturer. *American Educational Research Journal*, 1977, *14*, 449–57.

Worchel, P. Anxiety and repression. *Journal of Abnormal and Social Psychology*, 1955, *50*, 201–5.

Wyer, R. S. *Cognitive Organization and Change: An Information Processing Approach.* New York: John Wiley and Sons, 1975.

Zillig, M. Einstellung and Aussage. *Zeitsch. for Psychology,* 1928, *106,* 14–66.

Author Index

Subject Index